B IS FOR BURNOUT, NOT B*TCH

From Overdrive to Thrive A-Z

Dana Mahina

Copyright © 2023 Dana Mahina

Published by: Dana Mahina, LLC

All rights reserved. No part of this book may be reproduced or transmitted in any form or by any means, electronic or mechanical, including photocopying, recording, or by any information storage and retrieval system, without written permission of the author, except for the inclusion of brief quotations in a review.

ISBN: 979-8-9891298-0-5 (eBook)
       979-8-9891298-1-2 (Paperback)

Praise for "B is for Burnout"

I hope that every woman who feels like they are on a speeding train to burnout has a chance to sit down and read the wisdom in this book. This is it, ladies. This is your call to action. Dana Mahina presents an actionable guide to all women about how to stop living – and burning out – for everyone else and start prioritizing and living a joyful life for YOU.

~Karen Salmansohn, Bestselling Author of *Instant Calm*

From A to Z, Dana Mahina delivers ideas to make your life better. Read this snappy little book for the tough love -- and the fun.

~Laura Vanderkam, author of *I Know How She Does It*

Burnout can only occur when you care so much about your service to others (at work, at home, and everywhere in between) that you are willing to set yourself on fire in order to keep others warm. No. More. Dana Mahina gets this. She's been there. She's come through the fire and wants every other woman to find their way out. This book is a call to action for the women who understand that seeking joy and seeding responsibility are not mutually exclusive. Our time is now.

~Erin Gallagher, CEO and Founder of intersectional gender equity consultancy Ella; Creator of the Hype Women Movement and host of the Hype Women Podcast

Dana Mahina empowers working women with tools to manage, prevent, and crush burnout. The same tools that made her a success in corporate America, despite bureaucracy and the ridiculous expectations put on women throughout the world.

~Marsha Posner Williams,
Emmy and Golden Globe Winning Producer

In "B is for Burnout, Not Bitch," Dana Mahina kicks stereotypes to the curb, empowering women to recharge their batteries, embrace failure, and confidently say "No" like a boss. She's not just talk; she's walked the burnout walk and lived to tell the tale. This book isn't a snooze fest; it's your escape plan from Burnout City. It has all the secrets to unlock authenticity, set boundaries, and strut confidently. Ready to light your inner fire and rewrite the women's rulebook? Crack open this book, and your journey from burnout to ignition is a go. Read alphabetically or dance to your beat—it's your journey, your rules.

Daisy Auger-Dominguez, Author of *Inclusion Revolution: The Essential Guide to Dismantling Racial Inequity in the Workplace* and former Chief People Officer at Vice Media

"B Is for Burnout Not Bitch" is not just a book. It's an experience. And it's one that all women (and non-binary humans who have been conditioned to be/are perceived as women) MUST have as a resource for three reasons. 1 - It pulls the curtain back on the absurd expectations bestowed onto us that many of us have experienced, but few of us talk about. 2 - It gives you permission to be and expand into the biggest, baddest version of yourself unapologetically. 3 - It gives clear examples and tools for getting there. I don't just want to survive. I want to continue to thrive, and if you do, too, this book is for you!

~Jupiter F. Stone, Video Producer and Social Strategist

FREE GIFT AND FREEBIES FOR MY READERS

Get gifts and future deals by joining us on the journey to crush burnout! Sign up for our newsletter and get your Free Gift now, a one-page Frameable A-Z Work-Life Thriving Guide for Overachieving Women:

As women, we have enough going on in our lives, and sometimes, we need a visual reminder to stay out of the Burnout Zone!

Table of Contents

Foreword 1
My Story 7
Lessons from the Pandemic 19
A is for Authenticity –Finding the Real YOU 23
B is for Burnout Brought to You by Boundaries
 – And the Lack of Them 29
C is for Confidence 37
D is for Delegate Without Remorse– Overachieving Women
 Have a Hard Time with This 41
E is for Energy– Recharging After Burnout 45
F is for Failing– Not All Failures are Created Equal 51
G is for Gratitude 57
H is for Help –And Why We Suck At Asking for It 65
I is for Independence 69
J is for Joy 73
K is for Kyndrness 81
L is for Leadership– The 5 DIYs of Being a Good Leader 89
M is for Motivation – Matching My Time with Your Effort 95
N is for NO – Practice Saying It 99
O is for Opportunities– Created by Outsourcing 105
P is for Productivity 109
Q is For Questions – The Killer of Assumptions and
 Teacher of Root Cause 115
R is for Reality – Fact vs. Fiction 121

S is for Self-love 127

T is for Trust – But Verify 133

U is for Unity – Seek to Understand Before Being Understood 137

V is for Value 141

W is for Wait for It – Power of Pause 145

X is for X-factor 149

Y is for YOU! 153

Z is for the Zone 157

Acknowledgments 161

Dedication

To Burned Out Women EVERYWHERE!!!

Foreword

Women are mislabeled.

When we're stressed, we're unreasonable.

When we're ambitious, we don't know our place.

When we ask for help, we're needy, lazy, or manipulative.

It is complete and utter bullshit.

Have you ever asked a woman who appears to "have it all" how she is doing? They either insist they are fine, even though it's clear they are coming apart at the seams, or just this one caring question sends her over the edge into a puddle of gratitude because someone actually cares. This overachieving and superwoman mentality comes with a price. And the price is different for every woman.

For me, the price was pneumonia that would reoccur 2-4 times per year. The delusion that this was standard operating procedure for women like me culminated in a postpartum depression suicide attempt 23 years ago. I'll share more of my story later, but for now, know this:

- NO! I am NOT a crazy bitch. I am a woman who asks for what she deserves.

- NO! I am NOT a boss bitch. I am a woman who knows her value.

- NO! I am NOT bitchy. I am fed up and BURNED OUT.

And so are you!

You may not notice it because it's probably your norm.

Think hard. Are you constantly running on near empty? Do you have a cyclical sickness that pops its head up at the most inconvenient of times? Do you keep thinking, "If I can just get these couple of things done, I'll be back on track. That'll solve everything?"

If you answered yes to even one of these questions, you are probably burned out – or well on your way to becoming burned out.

Not to be too cliché, but the first step is admitting it. Admit that maybe how you have been running your life is not the best way for you. Admit that perhaps you are stuck in a cycle, thinking everyone else is operating just like you. It's a fallacy and not a reason to continue to kill yourself to do it all.

Just because every other woman around you is burning out doesn't mean you have to! Let's all grow together and help each other conquer and *prevent* burnout!

We often talk about burnout like it's a simple fact of life. Oh yeah, everyone burns out eventually. Just take a two-week break, "recharge," and come back and do it again until you, once again, burn out.

It's a stupid, vicious cycle.

We need to accept that burnout is a disease—a dis-ease. You are not at ease when you are burned out. You need to make conscious choices to prioritize your well-being and happiness to cure it. And I mean, all the time. Not just during your two-week vacation.

I'm telling you, it's the only cure.

This thriving women's guide to work-life design will show you how to go from burnout to being on fire for YOURSELF. The same way that I did just two short years ago. Without the guilt, overwhelm, and stress.

Today, I am thriving and teaching thousands of other women how to do the same for themselves. Together, we are stronger. Together, we are leaders. Together, we are trailblazers. We are charting a new course for future women to follow that ensures the quest for success will happen in sustainable, achievable, and glorious new ways. That, until now, we have felt were completely elusive, only for the rich and famous and, well, total bullshit!

Welcome! We are going to take care of you from A-Z.

Like the late great Louise Hay, we will also list the high-level practices from A-Z.

In the A-Z work-life thriving guide for overachieving women, you will discover:

A is for Authenticity – Finding the Real YOU

B is for Burnout Brought to You by Boundaries – And the Lack of Them

C is for Confidence

D is for Delegate without Remorse – Overachieving Women Have a Hard Time with This

E is for Energy – Recharging After Burnout

F is for Failing – Not All Failures Are Created Equal

G is for Gratitude

H is for Help – And Why We Suck At Asking For It

I is for Independence

J is for Joy

K is for Kyndrness

L is for Leadership – The 5 DIYs of Being a Good Leader

M is for Motivation – Matching My Time with Your Effort

N is for No – Practice Saying It

O is for Opportunities – Created by Outsourcing

P is for Productivity

Q is for Questions – The Killer of Assumptions and Teacher of Root Cause

R is for Reality – Fact vs. Fiction

S is for Self-love

T is for Trust – But Verify

U is for Unity – Seek to Understand Before Being Understood

V is for Value

W is for Wait for It – Power of Pause

X is for X-factor

Y is for YOU!

Z is for the Zone

Suggestions on how to get the most out of this book:

1. Read it chapter by chapter, sequentially.

2. Read it progressively, starting where you are struggling or where you want to go. But something is missing. Discover a tool or a tip you can use or a trap you should avoid.

3. Do the first method and then, as needed, revisit chapters via the second method.

Choose whichever method works best for you to digest the content of this book. This book is here to help you in whatever way you wish to be supported.

My Story

Now, let's back up for a minute, back to 2014.

Like you, I was trying to make adjustments to my work-life design. I knew that the perpetual quest for balance was bullshit. I had the battle scars to prove it from spending 11 years as a single mom with an international job, a spotty dating life, and wearing countless hats (none of which were cute, just sayin'), from friend to boss to community activist. I was like a daughter and sister to MANY (my parents had already passed away, and I lost my sister to ovarian cancer when I was only 20 and she was 25). I needed to change, or I wasn't just going to burn out; I was going to explode.

Then, the perfect storm hit – in a good way!

I received a glimpse into the kind of real partnership a divorcee might have with a man.

That's right, ladies, a real man. The kind that comes with a desire to recognize you for who you really are and the willingness to lend a hand and share his heart. What is this rare creature who can actually support and partner with the overachieving, high-functioning, and, more often than not, burned-out woman?

Today, he is my husband. My second and final. And that's a fact.

When we met and explored the idea of being together, I was no fool.

I'd had a toxic marriage and had turned myself into a human pretzel to please my ex (the biological father to my daughters). This new guy was going to pass MANY tests to make it into my Promised Land. I put him through the proverbial ringer before introducing him to my daughters, who were, at the time, 11 and 14 and in total hormone hell. Remember those days as young teenage women? Intensely emotional. Sometimes rational. Sometimes, not at all. Everything at that time in a woman's journey is hyper-sensitive and completely overwhelming.

Imagine, for a moment, coming into their lives as a new man. Not their dad and not a dad himself. And I was striking out on my own to start my own business. To say that it was a rough time for everyone is a massive understatement.

Something had to give. So, here's how I handled it. Feel free to quote me if you're overwhelmed with work, friends, and/or family.

I told him, right as I'm telling you now, in **no uncertain terms,** that I was NOT his mother or his therapist. HAHA! I really said it.

Although this was early on in our very new relationship, he was so sweet and patient but clearly perplexed by this edict of mine. He has an incredible nature and simply smiled and nodded, "Got it—not my mother, not my therapist."

Over the coming months and years, he would occupy the Free Space on my life's bingo card. He would prove to me over and over that he had what it took to partner me and stepparent our little women. Flash forward to today, nine years later, and they are VERY close. I'm convinced that they like him more than me… which actually works out well for all of us as I get a break, and he lends a male perspective and is a positive male role model in their lives that my "Wasband" doesn't provide. Most importantly, together, we are simply better.

So, if you want to harmonize your work-life, foundational element number one is to get your house in order!

If you're entering into a relationship of any depth, DO NOT compromise on the things that bring you the most joy and help you be your most productive self. Be super strategic about what you both do best, and, pretty please, I implore you to look at and really delve into the value of your relationships. Are you bringing out the best in each other? Are you sharing the load for all the things that need to take place on the daily in terms of your strengths and weaknesses, and vice versa for your partner? If they are not your clone, your project, or your wounded bird to heal and fix, they will change your life forever. And, in my case, he came with something really big. (Not that!!! Well, maybe that too… But that's not what I'm talking about right now. Sheesh!)

He came with another B! Benefits!

Now, I'm not suggesting you run out and marry someone just because their benefits package is awesome.

It goes right back to the fact that burnout for women is often the byproduct of hyper-achieving in order to provide. We are so driven to provide for our loved ones, extended family, and even friends that we work ourselves into a fever pitch. We don't see the creative options available to us. Even if you're beyond burnout as you read this, I promise there are options for you to explore.

In my case, going onto my partner's benefits for myself and my kids lowered my fear of risk and empowered me to take the leap to go out on my own as an author, leadership coach, and podcaster/speaker. What is available to you right now that you have brushed aside because it feels too good to be true or seems to be a "handout," but your pride won't let you accept it?

Take a step back to evaluate the creative and imaginative ways that you can get out of the burnout cycle where those who love and know you best are questioning your "bitchtude." Are you able to ask for help? Are you willing to make a trade-off? Are you considering sharing the load with someone you trust? Look to your inner circle of loved ones. Angels in our lives sometimes show up in mysterious ways. They may be a partner or best friend, sister or brother, neighbor or acquaintance. Doesn't matter. Take inventory, ladies. Sometimes, the only way to conquer the B is to outsource. More on that in Chapter O — Opportunities Created by Outsourcing.

Now, let's flash forward to 2016—the year of epic change.

We got married, and I quit my job as President/CEO of a professional services company without... wait for it... another job!

I was jumping off the cliff. This time, towards what I really wanted.

Me – as the boss of me.

I was a proven leader, a developer of other leaders and teams, and pretty strategic and insightful about running successful businesses. I mean, shit, I had two successful exits under my belt- helping other founders and leaders get to retirement. So, with my beloved hubby, two growing women to keep raising, and three rescue dogs, this was it.

I began by coaching others, both men and women, to redesign their busy lives. And I learned with them! I worked with private clients and teams to up-level their leadership, business, and overall lives for the better. At the same time, I, too, was making active trade-offs, sometimes monthly, weekly, and even daily.

I was making plans that I considered to be future "proofed." Meaning I was setting goals and making choices that I knew would pay off in terms of energetic dividends, as well as increasing my joy and ensuring that all the ways I give, spend time, effort, and energy would return the value I was giving in exchange for the value I was receiving.

I started to redefine the way I measure value. I started loosely tracking all the hats I was wearing, where I spent the majority of my time, effort, and energy over the 168 hours in the week that we all possess.

That's right, ladies, we cannot buy more time. And it isn't a use-it-or-lose-it situation. It's basic math.

24 hours per day x 7 days per week =168 hours in one week.

In 2020, I launched my podcast, today known as *Work-Life Harmonized*. Ironically, this was the same day the World Health Organization declared the pandemic.

Since then, the world has experienced a whirlwind of uncertainty, fear, and doubt. The pandemic changed the world as we knew it. But it did teach us as women to NEVER waste a crisis, illness, or time of total upheaval. We must face the dragon. We must learn to embrace the dragon. And ultimately, we must make the dragon our pet instead of our peeve.

The expectations that high-achieving and overachieving women place on ourselves, ideally, will be changed forever when it comes to how we show up for ourselves, our beloved families, friends, communities, and workplaces. We were already born smart. Now, we must be SMARTER when consciously choosing the life we want to lead and the legacy we want to leave behind for our daughters and their daughters, our nieces, and any next-gen person who identifies as female.

The art of actually stopping to choose what you want, how you want it, where you want it, and when, as well as with whom you want it, is the way to achieve the life you've always dreamed of.

It is NOT that you haven't tried hard enough. You've worked your ass off. ALWAYS. That's right, I'm talking to you! It is like looking in the mirror. You spot it, you got it. BOOM.

I am you, and you are me, and we are we. We are the overachieving women who have had enough!

It is NOT that you haven't dreamed big enough. You've done vision boards, joined LeanIn circles, and participated in every form of therapy from behavioral to group to new age. We all continue to latch onto Oprah, Brené Brown, Gabrielle Bernstein, Glennon Doyle, and even the male version of these wildly successful, inspirational up-levelers in the game of life, only to come up short for ourselves.

Why? Well, it's simple. We put ourselves last.

We choose to do this, and it's time we learn to break the cycle and head toward freedom. If not now, when? Won't you join me? Let me show you exactly how to do it. It won't be easy. But it can be simple. As long as we don't complicate it with guilt, prioritizing others' needs ahead of our own, or miss opportunities to put ourselves first.

I'm talking about conscious settling—not settling, as in settling for less. But settling, as in settling down and in. When it comes to conscious settling, we simply must learn how to Settle Smarter.

Let's face it. We are already smart. Smart enough to be reading this book, searching for answers and self-improvement across our most precious life facets. So, what gives? Well, you do!

Let's look at what's different today about the ways in which we MUST settle, especially women and people who haven't had their voices heard, perhaps ever. Women of color, the LGBTQ+ community, and anyone who does not fit the current standards of "the norm," I am revealing my best life's work and building an action plan for YOU!

Wait, you, my favorite reader, is asking, "What happened to you, Dana, since the Pandemic struck?"

Oh! I am so very glad you asked. That's a very happy ending and a new beginning.

In November 2020, we relocated permanently to an island! For real.

We live on Kauai and have yet to experience any flavor of island fever. When that perfect storm I spoke about earlier hit me, it was time to hit the reset button on my life once and for all.

Not everyone needs or wants to relocate to an island. This was a way for me to reinvent the life I always wanted, yet I was sure I could not have.

This life is slower, way slower than the rush of Silicon Valley, which is measured in titles and electric cars. This life is free from smoke-filled seasons that really screw up someone's quality of life when they suffer from asthma. This life is for swimming in warm, open waters, immersing in deep, ancient culture, and hula. (My hips don't lie either, Shakira! They don't want to move that much, though.)

Of course, I realize and own that I am in an enviable position. I can work from almost anywhere in the world. My business is my passion, and I'm paid well for it.

Here's the secret that I will share with you right now. Hyper-achieving and overachieving women who have led the way for many years on behalf of their families, communities, and even their true selves have earned the right to choose the type of life they want. I don't believe everyone deserves it, like a birthright or entitlement. Haters gonna hate. So, go ahead and blow up my DMs if you must. I simply don't buy it.

Overachieving women are one of the world's most precious resources. We are an asset. Yes, sometimes we are a pain in the ass. But we are NOT bitches. Most of us are burned out and have little to nothing left to give. We are one cold away from full-blown pneumonia.

The best way for me to help you get what you want, where you want it (island or otherwise), when you want it, how you want it, and with whom you desire to have "it" is to show you EXACTLY how I did it. And how I am protecting what I've created for myself each day.

It all starts with Why. I'm not the first author to talk about "discovering your why." I have Simon Sinek'd myself so many times. My clients are tired of me saying, "What's the why of your business? What's the why behind your mission? Why do you exist? Personally? Professionally?" Why, Why, Why.

That is NOT what I'm talking about in terms of why. I love you, Simon, no offense intended. Your work has helped me and countless others, obviously. This type of "why" is all about YOU. You and only you. You when no one else is around. You when no one outside of yourself influences you when allowing yourself the exquisite pleasure of this particular "why" discovery without guilt, without remorse, and without a lack of confidence or artificial boundaries that scold you for daring to ask why in the first place. "You don't deserve this luxury." Except for one critical thing: YOU do deserve it! Why? Because you have earned it.

Now, in order to live the life you really want, brought to you by the power of why, we need to keep unpacking all the other secrets that will fuel your efforts. I'm talking about proven decision-making tools that, once understood and in your grasp, you will deploy over and over and over again for the rest of your life – and many lifetimes if you believe that sort of thing. I certainly do!

Since moving to the island of Kauai, I have witnessed no less than one miracle, 50+ cases of extreme serendipity/synchronicity, and, even more importantly, learned how to wrap the Spirit of Aloha around myself and now, all of you. If you have ever traveled to any of the Hawaiian Islands or any place in the world where you feel totally at ease, at peace, and in flow, especially if you are an overachiever on the verge of another burnout, then you know what I'm living.

Let's take a moment to feel what stepping off the plane in a tropical location is like. The air is thick with velvety moisture, there is an undeniable smell of fresh flowers, and you are drawn in to breathe the air slowly, purposefully, and knowingly. Peace is on the way. You're a smart, creative, kickass woman. You can use any similar example you like here; it may be a retreat in the mountains, a drive up to the snow, or a bath filled with Epsom salts where no one asks you for anything for a full 15 minutes. They don't scream your name, and your phone isn't buzzing away, alerting you to the latest crisis. You are simply in a state of well-being. Create these opportunities for yourself.

Ahhhhhh. Feel the decompression. Smell what's sweet in the air.

Let It All Go.

For me, the feeling of peace, total connection to being on this earth, and living a life of authenticity is and always will be located on the island of

Kauai. This will not be a realistic option for many of you. Or you aren't extremely interested in completely transforming how and where you live. That is OK, that is so totally OK. Do you know why? You will do it your way, and it will be good, and then it will be great, and over time, you will decompress, put out the dumpster fire that is burnout, and start to be your most joyful and fulfilled self.

And I'm going to help you.

How did I know this was it? What made me take the leap? Does it have to be that extreme? I'm so glad that you asked me all of these questions. I get them all the time, even from strangers.

I knew this was it because I had traveled here 10+ times throughout the years, and it is the one and only place on earth (and I've been around!) where I feel at ease and unplugged after deplaning. Here, it never took me 1-3 days to decompress and get into "vacation mode." Here, I didn't find excuses to check one more email before eating dinner with my family or allowing myself to go snorkeling. Here, I connect with my own sense of self, purpose, and well-being in a way that shows others that it is more than OK to put my own needs first. Here, I am helping others in ways my spread-too-thin-self could never accomplish. Here, I feel seen, heard, and known. Here, I am free to be myself. Fuck the critics.

I took the leap like most overachieving women do things—all at once. When that perfect storm of crushing it at work yet not being fully recognized, appreciated, or fairly compensated hit, coupled with the smoke-filled months from the California wildfires, having a partner who provided benefits, minimizing my risk, I knew it was time to bet on myself and leap.

Yes, moving to a fairly remote island with serious supply chain issues and different cultural norms and barriers would appear extreme to some.

Ladies, this is NOT cocktails with umbrellas every day and idyllic weather 24/7 paradise. Like all situations, a vacation is a vacation for a reason. It's a break from the action and an escape for many burned-out women to recharge their batteries to get right back into the hamster wheel. This, for me, is not that. This is not a permacation or staycation or workcation or any "cation." This is my life. It's a serious adjustment, filled with up-leveling life lessons, super-conscious trade-offs, strategic planning, and ongoing decision-making. Most days include compromises, discoveries, and growth. This type of life move is not for everyone.

What follows in the next 26 chapters is designed to help you create a life for you and only you, from A to Z. You will understand why it is vital to put yourself first and what that looks like for you.

You will also learn how to have energizing time for yourself with as little or as grand of life changes as you desire. You will navigate your relationships and learn who will aid, assist, and augment you and who needs to be kicked to the curb. I mean it! It's gonna happen.

You will learn where you really need to be to live your best life in moments, days, weeks, months, and potentially years.

And finally, I really do mean FINALLY, you will learn when to make these changes in a way that's divinely timed in terms of your Joy, Productivity (energy added vs. depletion), and Value.

Together, we will do it. I've got your back. I'm in your corner. And I have enough space, time, and lessons learned to help you apply it all as the wind beneath your wings. Let's get ready to take off.

Lessons from the Pandemic

Before we get started, I want to talk about the pandemic because we all learned so much from it.

Career

Before COVID-19 and the uncertainty of the pandemic (remember the toilet paper crisis?), we went into the office to work. We never truly considered that we would be as, if not more, productive working from home, sometimes on top of one another. And now, we've done it. We survived the worst of the pandemic. We all have scratches, scars, and wounds but are ultimately resilient, informed, and, therefore, powerful. Many of us have more choices and freedom to work in hybrid ways, both in and out of office workplaces. I see talented people in the driver's seat more than ever before. We are digital nomads and risk-taking solopreneurs. We are changing how we lead companies in truly transformational ways. **This** is acting SMARTER!

Family

Before COVID-19, we (and women in particular) tackled every role we play by wearing multiple and competing hats – all the time. Juggling life's roller coaster of work and kids and partners and bears, oh friggin' my! Today, we are learning to heed the warning signs. Family obligations that create giant piles of guilt are NOT joy-producing, nor *productive, let alone equitable in terms of the value equation (both giving and receiving).*

Consider what one of my podcast guests had to say: *"Invisible work: invisible because it may be unseen and unrecognized by our partners, and also because those of us who do it may not count or even acknowledge it as work... despite the fact that it costs us real-time and significant mental and physical effort with no sick days or benefits."*

—Eve Rodsky, "Fair Play: A Game-Changing Solution for When You Have Too Much to Do"

Friendships

During COVID-19, we truly got smarter about who our real friends are and who they are not. When you cannot literally see, touch, or be with your "friends," superficially or in a very close-knit way, what rises to the top? The cream of the crop. The friends that have your back are your ride-or-die and who you show up for equally. They endured the pandemic and became your closest tribe members and allies because the effort it took to maintain relationships was enormous. Everything was on display. EVERYONE saw our dirty laundry, unwashed hair, and rambunctious children and pets right on the screen. Can you say Zoom fatigue? Real friends from your inner circle became invaluable to you and you to them. The SMARTER lesson learned here is that designing a life with a tight core group of friends, 1-3 and no more, is sanity-saving, soul-empowering, and, at times, the only way to navigate our busy lives.

Community

What the hell was that during COVID-19? Given how individual and personal community is, this facet is already the most difficult to define. And thanks to the pandemic, all the previous ways we showed up in and for our communities vanished. POOF. We had to start over. What is a community? How do you play an active or inactive role within a community? Is it all digital and germ-free now, or is it something else entirely? Like the start-up I helped launch, where we set out to teach the world how to be Kyndr. (Check out the app if you're sick of toxic social media!) What about podcasts and social communities where we support each other via total strangers who feel like home? Once again, our belief systems are being tested and now have been blown apart. Blood is still not thicker than water. Our friends and community members are becoming our extended family in ways that both challenge and support us. This is way smarter.

And finally, and ideally NEVER last, well-being

The workaholics, overachievers, and perfectionists of the pre-pandemic world were already on full tilt. Working from home under extreme pressure to perform and outlast everyone else in order to survive created 24/7 shops out of humans. And who worked the hardest at work and in the home yet saw the deepest cuts in employment? You guessed it. Women! Until we had no choice. We became way smarter and started creating space by designing time savers and joy-producing practices that today we will fight to maintain, even when the fight is an internal one with ourselves.

> *"Hard work is important. So are play and nonproductivity.*
> *My worth is tied not to my productivity but to my existence.*
> *I am worthy of rest."*
> —Glennon Doyle, "Untamed"

A

is for Authenticity – Finding the Real YOU

"There is power in allowing yourself to be known and heard, in owning your unique story, in using your authentic voice."
—Michelle Obama

A is for Authenticity – with a side of Aloha magic.

I'm not going to bullshit you. You've already had enough of that, or you wouldn't be reading this book.

Authenticity is an ideal and a tricky one at that. We all strive to be authentic, but your work, your family, and even society as a whole may be telling you that your authentic self will not be accepted, will make it difficult to work with you, or will simply burden the people around you.

Screw 'em. Screw them all.

We *need* to be our authentic selves if we're going to become all we can be – and be truly, actually happy with where we are in life.

Consider this incredible woman named Betsy. She was already an accomplished woman when I met her. She saw me give a talk to around a thousand women (and a few good men) on ways to build confidence by making conscious trade-offs and dumping the stuff that doesn't serve you. And before you ask, yes, that includes dumping people, places, and things. She found me after my talk and hired me to coach her.

Why would a woman with such advanced levels of academic acronyms from Ivy League and progressive universities, an esteemed professor, and a financial services wizard need help finding and using her authentic voice? And if *she's* struggling, where does that leave the rest of us?

It became crystal clear after one discovery call.

This woman, who had sat at the Hubble telescope and ran algorithms for hedge funds, was unsure of herself.

She didn't have the courage to start her own company. It had been her dream for years after working in brutal, male-dominated careers. But she needed way more than a pep talk to pull the trigger.

She needed to *act as if*.

What does that mean? It means you have to assume the positive and assume the win. Try it with the belief that you will succeed, even – and especially – when you're not sure of success.

Now, back to you, what are you afraid of right now?

What about your true authentic self are you hiding, sheltering, or burying deep down within yourself because your partner, society, or the crappy PTA club is finger-wagging at you?

Stop hiding. Start acting as if.

Acting as if works like this:

Act as if you already have the job you want, the partner you desire, or the best friend you dream of. Start today! Design your own mini experiment, grab a friend or loved one to hold you accountable, and get after it. Give yourself a minimum of three months to dive in. Really go for it. Find a way to create the experience you believe in your heart that you want.

You may need to volunteer, work a few more hours for no additional pay, or stop unwanted monthly lunches with those judgmental, naysayer ladies. Make the change today. Start now, and test, test, test.

Once you've tried it on for fit, you'll know much more about whether you want to be promoted, start your own shop on ETSY, or spend three more hours per week with yourself and no one else, just lunching alone.

This concept is NOT to be confused with *Fake it 'til you make it* or become it. Most of you have at least heard of the infamous Mary Kay lady who started the multi-level marketing movement for women who drive pink Cadillacs and sell cosmetics from their homes and all that jazz. I tried it in college and quickly failed by selling back all my products, a one-time event that means you're out of the pink sisterhood forever.

What I took away from the experience was learning about the authentic woman whose autobiography was required reading. She shared her concept for all women to "Fake it 'til you make it." This was later adapted into a viral video phenomenon by Harvard Business School's very own Amy Cuddy, who modernized the quote into, "Fake it 'til you become it," sending thousands of women around the world into power-posing positions. She scientifically proved that we could lift our hormonal levels, increasing testosterone and decreasing cortisol, significantly improving our ability to act as if we are fully ourselves even if we haven't become it. But we can, by taking small risks and experimenting until who we really are becomes one with who we were born to be.

We go from acting as if to authenticating our own identity—no algorithm required. And the real beauty of this approach is that anyone can do it. This tool is available to you right now.

Let's get back to our story about Betsy. So, here she was on the precipice of her own authentic mission to truly become who she knew she was born to be. However, there were simply too many "That was then vs. this is now" moments in her way.

This lesson became vital for Betsy to learn. She was in a new role in a totally different industry. She was trying on what it felt like to lead a team inside a tech start-up before embarking on launching her own. Why? Because she had to experience what it's like to become just brave and experienced enough to know what she wanted for herself. The coaching lesson for her became "try before you buy," or invest, in her case. And her investment became significant: time, effort, energy, money, and resources.

Today, she runs a game-changing social media platform that focuses on positive interactions, highlighting authentic human interactions and the very best creator journeys possible for like-minded, good-hearted, and soul-based individuals who are here on this planet to do good! Yes, you read that right. It's a social media platform created to be the complete opposite of the toxic wasteland of all the others. See Chapter K is for Kyndrness, to learn more about Betsy, her journey, and her app, Kyndr.

And finally, let's talk about the depth and breadth of the word that is a concept, a way of living, and more: Aloha.

I thought up and down about the best way to describe Aloha. It is so much more than a greeting and way to say goodbye. I finally asked my very good friend Kauilani Kahalekai – who is a musician, kumu (teacher) of Hawaiian practices, kahu (ordained minister), sits on the Kupuna Board and Burial Council of Kauai, as well as the Kaneiolouma Heiau Board and the Advisory Board for Land and Water Resources Stories of Kauai, and is an ambassador of Aloha for Hawaii – if she knew of a good way to describe Aloha to my readers, who may have never been to Hawaii.

She thought for a moment and then said, "Aloha is something that you feel and you give, and it makes you feel warm. And the more you practice it, the warmer you feel inside and the brighter your outside. The indigenous people of Hawaii want you to know that the Aloha Spirit lives in all of us."

The Big So What?

So, it's hard to be authentic. That's why being a solopreneur or founder of something isn't for everyone. And, for women, it's still the minority, around 39%. But in order to really go for what you want and get rid of what you don't, it takes authenticity. Becoming your true self will happen with planning, understanding, and experimenting. Try it. You may find that you like the real you best. And while you're at it, no matter where you are in the world reading this, try adopting the practice of ALOHA.

B

is for Burnout
Brought to You by Boundaries
– And the Lack of Them

"When we fail to set boundaries and hold people accountable, we feel used and mistreated."

—Brené Brown

B is for Burnout brought to you by boundaries – and the lack of them.

Establish them now!

"But Dana Mahina," says the angry bubble above your head about to explode in reproachful *hmphs*. "I already feel like a bitch, and I'm being accused by everyone around me that I *am* a bitch. I'm reading this damn book because I'm totally burned out, have been burned out off and on for years, and now, you're giving me another to-do on my ever-growing list, which is making me even bitchier. *I* don't even want to be around me any longer, not even for a minute."

Okay, dear reader. Allow me the pleasure of leading you away from the edge. One foot in front of the other. That's right. Microstep your way back and know that establishing clear and distinct boundaries will de-bitch even the bitchiest bitches. And remember, YOU ARE NOT actually a bitch (most likely). You are *burned out*.

According to a recent study by Forbes, women are suffering from an "Exhaustion Gap." According to the article, women are experiencing a massive 68% feeling of burnout post-pandemic, fueled by work-life imbalance and pressure to perform at work and beyond.[1] Even the fight against burnout is causing more burnout. So, what gives?

Well, you do. You give and give and give until there's nothing left for yourself. Not for those who really need you and definitely not for the people you'd like to support. There is simply not enough energy to go around.

Let's start with the most basic yet critical, THE tool of all the tools in my Toolkit of Freedom—Individual Core Values. This is the starting place to establish the guardrails for your life that define the boundaries you must set for yourself to become increasingly free. These are fairly wide-open spaces where in between, there is room to breathe and try new things – even safe-to-fail experiments (See Chapter A is for Authenticity for ways to experiment).

Now, please take 5-10 minutes to answer the following:

1. What is your true North?

    In other words, your guiding life principle. This can be integrity, faith in humanity, family first, and so on.

2. If you were a product, a service, a widget, or a gadget, what would make you unique? What would be your marketplace differentiator?

---

[1] https://www.forbes.com/sites/kimelsesser/2022/03/14/women-are-suffering-from-an-exhaustion-gap-according-to-new-study/?sh=504f3e6737b3

This can be boldness, willingness to lend a hand to complete strangers, out-of-the-box creativity, etc.

3. What is your number one deal breaker? The line that can NEVER be crossed with you, or else!

You may say never lie, cheat, or steal from me, hurt my family, insult my intelligence, etc.

Boundary Number 1

Now that you are equipped with your individual core values, it's time to set the initial boundaries to save you from ongoing burnout. This is the first tool I have for you that will establish, re-establish, and create energy where exhaustion lived before.

Look at or think about your answer to the first question above. If you said integrity is your truest north, this will become your first clear-cut boundary.

Still not tracking? Let me simplify. Any job, "soulmate," bestie, or pet project not operating within your definition of integrity has to GO! BYE! Take out the trash; it stinks.

Boundary Number 2

Now you're cooking! This boundary comes from double and triple checking how you spend your time. If what makes you truly unique (from question two above) is that you are super creative and out of the box, and yet, if the job you have is a static 9-5, totally coloring inside the lines, boring as hell, you can do it in your sleep type gig, you're in the wrong place! Quit today (if you're financially able to and are cool with burning bridges)!

Either way, I want you to create a plan up or a plan out. This is how I became a President/CEO in the hyper-competitive world of Silicon Valley. It doesn't matter that once I got there, I didn't want it anymore – read my first book, *Stop Settling, Settle Smart,* for more on that crazy life lesson. I had to make eight consecutive moves over a twenty-five-year period. Some of those moves were moving up inside companies via promotions, acting as if, and pushing my way into roles that weren't made for "girls like me." Others were by leaving good paying, not super hard to do any longer, leadership positions in order to up-level my skills, exposure, and experiences: moving out.

In my case, I changed titles like underwear for several years and did not stay anywhere longer than six years. I tasted all the flavors of the working rainbow, from start-up to Fortune 500 and everything in between. You know, today, people change jobs on average every 3-5 years and careers three times in a lifetime. Who knew I was a norm?

Certainly not my family; they thought my ADD had gotten the better of my sanity.

Ladies, it was sanity-saving.

Boredom is death for women like us. We do not stagnate or phone it in; we have to grow, learn, and rise. It's essential to our own well-being and the contributions we are born to make, which is why things are so paradoxical for high-functioning women. We want to stand out and be the best versions of ourselves, and yet, this is what drives us to burnout.

So, when you make these bold moves up or out, a big fat "AND" is at play here.

DO NOT – let me repeat that so I know you heard me – DO NOT kill yourself the first year. Pace yourself. The rapid pace you set in month one becomes a groove that feels an awful lot like sprinting a marathon. And you cannot sprint an entire marathon. You just can't, ladies. And most women work their asses off beyond what's human for the first year in a new role or company to establish themselves as vital players, stave off the hyper-competition, and tell themselves they are contributing their utmost.

The huge issue that fuels the burnout is that you are not only on fumes, hanging on by a thread, literally day-by-day-by-day, in a cycle that repeats until the weekend comes, which isn't rest and recuperation time. Oh no. Not you, my queens. You will do 72 errands, pay your bills, help a friend in need, go on a date with your partner, and sew a fabulous dinosaur costume for your kid's first school play. And now you've really done it to yourself because the masses of fans and foes expect it from you. You are expected to perform at an Olympic level from now to eternity.

It doesn't work like that. Not for long, anyway. You'll crash, get sick, or lose your shit on an unsuspecting barista on your third Starbucks run of the day for jet fuel.

And while we're on the topic of realistic pace-setting boundaries, 4-day weekends are a nap. A breather. NOT a long-term solution to burnout. You cannot rely on holidays and short vacations to make up for this feverish pace you're keeping.

You **cannot** be out of the box, creative, and imaginative when you are burned out. And how do you stave off burnout? With healthy, clear, and realistic boundaries. So, let's set them ASAP.

What are you waiting for? If you haven't thrown this book (or your Kindle) into the fire or out the window, we're really getting to know each other. Thank you. I love you. Let's keep going. It's only going to get better, I promise. Thousands of women have done it with these guiding principles and action steps, and so will you.

The Big So What?

When you take on a new role at work or change companies for good reason, pace yourself. Give it your 80%, not your 120%.

I am NOT saying do the bare minimum.

Women like to dance circles around others even when we're only operating at 80%. Our 80% is like other people's 100-120%. We are high achievers, major contributors, and highly valuable humans. Leave a little time for yourself and the others you love, will you? Sheesh.

I have coached many women on how to do this successfully, and it works every single time. When you set the pace with people in your life at work and at home, that becomes the "norm"—they expect this pace from you, and it's reasonable enough to pack a punch in terms of what you give. And you get something out of this, too. You get a life! It's the only one, goddess, so put the "u" back in value! This is easier with newer people, but stick with it, and the people already in your life will get with the program (or if they don't – dump 'em).

Finally, the third major guardrail of boundary setting to keep you from crashing is never ever ever EVER allowing anyone to cross your deal-breaker. That's correct, you heard me. Say it like this,

"I _____ (insert your name) will never ever ever EVER allow anyone who boldly, maliciously, and obnoxiously lies to my face for their personal gain to remain in my life."

This is just one clear example. If the deal-breaker doesn't fit, revisit the third question, adjust, and practice saying this mantra out loud. Try it while you drive or stick three Post-it notes wherever you see yourself often: mirrors or your computer monitor or magnet that shit to your fridge. Do it!

Now, feel the space we've created. And you haven't even taken the action yet. Mostly, you've discovered where you stand. And you now have solid rationale for what boundaries are missing from your life and why.

Feel a little better?

Imagine now that you've locked these in and thrown away the key. These will be with you for the rest of your life, and they work!

They work for you, and you are a badass! You have energy. You have joy. And you have the most precious asset of all assets in the world! You. Have. TIME.

And always, and forever more, remember: the best way to avoid burnout is to choose how, when, where, with whom, what, and why you spend your time. (Want to figure it out right now? Take my quiz at https://dana.kyndrleaders.com/.)

Later, we will explore your level of Joy. That's right, Joy! With a capital J. Then we will assess together where your productivity lies (not just overachieving, multitasking hyper-efficiency, even though you are. You're reading this book, aren't you?).

In Chapter V, we will talk about the two-part equation that is value. The value you are giving and the value you are receiving.

Here goes: this is a doozy and the most important lesson of all my 30+ years in the world of work, single motherhood, now remarried, and all the hats we wear.

We do it to ourselves. We burn ourselves out.

We say yes when we really mean no. We feel bad, or even worse, guilty, about not helping a friend or a friend's friend or the friend of an old acquaintance who isn't even a friend. We take on other people's burdens, shit, even their responsibilities when we are already doing so much for others. We are putting ourselves and our own needs, health, and welfare dead last. Last! There are two simple words that I will now take my prescription pad out and write for you with unlimited refills so that you have it on the ready whenever you need it.

STOP IT.

The best way to "STOP IT" is to practice saying no. Go immediately to Chapter N is for NO! You will learn all there is to know about how and when to say no, why you must become an expert on the power of no, and most importantly, how to say no so people will listen. It works every time. Get ready to free yourself!

C
is for Confidence

"When the whole world is silent, even one voice becomes powerful... If people were silent, nothing would change... We were scared, but our fear was not as strong as our courage... They thought that the bullets would silence us, but they failed."
—Malala Yousafzai

C is for Confidence

Confidence is where I find most of the women I coach to be lacking, which is baffling! All these talented, smart women leaders, and they lack confidence?!?! It's nuts.

Well, no more. Not if I have anything to say about it.

The biggest key to building confidence is to learn, learn, learn.

Consume knowledge voraciously. Ask your boss, onboarding trainer, coworkers, and teammates relevant questions. Knowledge is power and will help you build up the confidence to tackle new problems and work toward your career goals.

Shadowing is a great way to learn and grow your confidence and career simultaneously. Focus on shadowing people who are one rung above you on the corporate ladder and whose job you find interesting.

The best way to continue to learn and build up your confidence is to practice where it's safe with a mentor (or a group of other like-minded and hearted women at various stages of their lives).

Mentors are the people who help guide you on your career path. Finding a mentor you respect and can ask career-related (and life) questions to is a great way to gain confidence.

I've only one mentor in my life who just happened to be my boss. And while he was my only true mentor, he impacted my life in a huge way.

Back in the day (a lot further back than I care to admit), when my children were very young, I told my mentor that I wanted to leave my office at 4:30 p.m. every day. I had (and still have) workaholic tendencies and I wanted to spend more time with my children. And he held me accountable! He would stand in the doorway of my office and tell me, "It's 4:30. Time for you to go home."

In the beginning, I would always try to push the time. Just a couple more emails. Just one more meeting. But he wouldn't let me. He would say, "Nope. Pack it up." And then loom ominously in my doorway until I did.

After a while, he didn't have to stand in my doorway.

Mentors don't always show up in that hierarchical way, however. When looking for a mentor, look for someone you respect and like, in a position you want to hold one day and in the industry you want to work. This will allow them to guide you, help you avoid pitfalls, and offer advice unique to your industry.

Asking someone to be your mentor is an incredibly daunting task at first. You may feel silly or worry about rejection. Put all those feelings aside!

Most people enjoy talking about their journeys and offering the wisdom they have built up over the years.

Now that you're learning and have a kick-ass mentor, I want you to build confidence by not trying to be perfect. You hear that? You are not allowed to strive for perfection.

But you can strive for permanence.

This may sound silly, but you need to practice handling tough situations or situations that make you uncomfortable. Whether that be delivering critical feedback or presenting a presentation to your boss.

And I don't mean wait for those things to pop up and learn as you go. That is going to happen anyway. I'm talking about proactively handling those situations by practicing them first by yourself and then with a friend or trusted peer.

Let's go with practicing giving critical feedback as an example. We struggle with this as women because we're terrified that we'll offend someone or won't be heard correctly.

First, practice the situation by standing in front of a mirror, pretending you are giving the person your critique. Watch yourself, your body language, and your facial expressions. The visual helps you to see what you may be subconsciously projecting. Are you crossing your arms? Are you fidgeting?

Once you have that, practice the situation with a friend or trusted peer. In this case, try to avoid family members because they may be more invested in the situation and have difficulty staying neutral and giving you unbiased feedback. You may also feel offended if a family member tells you your approach is wrong. Find someone who can give you honest feedback and stay unbiased when telling you what you're doing well and what you're doing poorly.

The Big So What?

Learn to listen to connect, NOT control. This is one of the most self-empowering, confidence-boosting techniques. As I say to my young adult daughters all the time, "Do you really, truly, honestly believe that you are in control? Really!? Did you *make* all of this? Did *you* create heaven and earth, plants and birds, womankind herself? Did you?"

If not, then what you do have is free will. You have, we all have, the power of choice! That's why we must use it wisely, situationally, and relatively day by day. Connect with people honestly and authentically and problem-solve from there. Practice the great and somewhat lost art of listening to connect, not control, and watch your confidence bloom as connections with others soar.

D
is for Delegate Without Remorse – Overachieving Women Have a Hard Time with This

"From what I've seen, it isn't so much the act of asking that paralyzes us--it's what lies beneath: the fear of being vulnerable, the fear of rejection, the fear of looking needy or weak. The fear of being seen as a burdensome member of the community instead of a productive one."

—Amanda Palmer

For many years, I've been perfecting my ability to delegate at work and at home. Sometimes, I find myself delegating out in my community and, occasionally, within my friend groups.

In this chapter, I will lay out all the ways to delegate efficiently and effectively without any remorse whatsoever.

This is not a fantasy; this is reality. Well, it's my reality, and soon, it will be yours too.

Once you learn to delegate without remorse, you will never go back to the way things were. Let me break it down for you.

1. It's always best to delegate with the person's individual core values and strengths in mind. You learned about this in Chapter

B, where I taught you about your individual core values. Use that same approach and exercise with those around you. If you have employees, start with them. Have this discussion with each employee individually, draw them out, and help them learn about themselves.

2. I strongly recommend one tool, and one tool only, for assessing people's core talents and skills. I have been administering the Clifton Strengths Finder Assessment for 17 years. I love it because it shows people quickly and in a non-invasive way what they love to do, what they are great at doing, and what they stink at. We all have top talents and blind spots. Why not fast-track things for yourself and others and learn what these are? That way, when delegating to others at work, divvying up the tasks for the kid's fundraiser, or even deciding who is taking which part in church events, you can delegate effectively and efficiently because you are informed.

3. Now that you know what the people are motivated by and driven towards (this is their North Star) and how cool and unique they are and, finally, armed with knowing these women's deal breakers, you will NOT delegate something to them that makes them uncomfortable, weirded out, or resentful.

The Big So What?

If you knew that you hit a bullseye every time you delegate, would you do it?

If you knew that the women in your life would actually enjoy being delegated to and, in exchange, may delegate to you in the same way, would you delegate more?

The remorse only happens when you delegate ineffectively to others who are overloaded, burning out, and people pleasers. This is NOT an awesome delegation strategy, and the tactics around this approach suck. It's time to master this skill, ladies. You can thank me later. Better yet, become a master delegator and teach others to do the same. Then hit me up on social media and tell me all about it so I can celebrate you. You can easily find me, so reach out and brag about yourself. Women aren't great at that anyway, so it's another practice ground for you. Let's go!

E

is for Energy
– Recharging After Burnout

*"Time is elastic. It stretches to accommodate
what we need or want to do with it. "*

— Laura Vanderkam

The best way to check-in with yourself periodically to determine your energy levels and how you are feeling right now is to use what I like to call *The Dial*. I use this tool when the women I'm helping seem depleted, bored, or distracted.

Introducing The Dial (0-100) or How You Doin'?

First, choose where you want to focus on assessing your energy (or a friend's if you're helping each other). Let's say that you choose to focus on family. On a scale of 0 – 100, where is your energy level right now? 0 = Nada, Nothing, None. 100 = could literally run the 100-yard dash in three seconds flat.

When you take your energy pulse using this dial, you are at 50. Not super energized or de-energized. It's a neutral and blasé place to be.

Now, ask yourself or a friend what it would take to be optimal. Is an 80 optimal for you? A 90? Try not to go for 100. Remember, it's exhausting and not sustainable to be on full tilt all the time. Did you see the movie "Molly's Game?" Shit, that terrified me. She is so smart and driven. Just because she applied her incredible skills to the game of poker and went DOWN in a blaze of glory doesn't make her a bad person, does it?

I digress.

Choose a realistic energy target. Next, ask: What would need to happen to go from a 50 to an 80? What has to change? What needs to start? How do other things need to stop?

After you explore this for a few minutes, take the dial quiz again. Are you still at a 50? Are you now at a 60? Most women find that their energy increases simply by exploring what works and doesn't and learning about what they want—what they really, really want. Are the Spice Girls still considered cool? Or vintage? I'll ask my 19- and 23-year-old daughters and let you know.

You now feel a little better. You have a little more energy simply from this exploratory discussion you're having. Imagine that. You haven't even made the changes to help your energy. Once you take action and put into place the shifts that will enhance your energy over time, your dial in this area of life will be fairly consistent and predictable. This, in turn, starts spilling into other areas of your life, such as work, marriage, volunteering, hanging with your pets, you name it.

Of course, you want extra credit; you're overachievers, after all. So, let's keep going.

Use *The Dial* across all key facets of life, friendships, career, community, and your own well-being. The same rules apply.

Before you know it, you will be a decisive, energy-producing, totally self-aware lady. Pass it on. We all need to create positive energy with and for the things and people we love. First and foremost for ourselves. Then, for those we love. IF, and only if, they are an energy-enhancing person in your life. Otherwise, they'll drag down your dial average. Gotta put yourself first. Me before we, bitches! The "putting on oxygen mask before helping others" analogies have been way over done.

The next tool I use with leaders is a reset on what many of us high achievers are doing. We have been wired to slow down *just enough* to speed up. This is bullshit and primarily taken from race car analogies, which don't work in real life.

I have never found anyone better to teach this concept of "when you feel the need to speed up, that is actually the time to slow it down" than Kimmi Werner from Maui. This 20-minute TEDx talk is something I have used hundreds of times with leaders. Watch the entire story. It's UNBELIEVABLE and worth the time to see what she does and who she does it with. Rated W for WOW WOW WOW, she teaches us why it is vital, and I mean literally VITAL, to do what feels unnatural and slow things down when you feel the acceleration need kick in. There is so much to be gained, learned, and healed when we slow down our motion. Things will come into focus, and new solutions will present themselves.

Okay, good work. Now that you're willing to slow down and have an informed point of view, let's make sure that you build a solid foundation before launching yourself, your team, your product, or all of the above off of that foundation. In order to do this, I teach this formula for success:

- 60% of your time MUST be spent on foundational items, blocking and tackling, daily tasks, and "stuff." These things include, but are not limited to, email, watering the plants, eating… you get the picture.

- 30% of your time MUST be spent pushing the limits, seeing around corners, and considering the future and what's to come. Examples here may include reading about market trends, experimenting with new recipes, running an extra mile, etc..

- 10% of your time MUST be spent on your moonshot! This is an area of your work, or more likely, big-hairy-audacious goal (known as a BHAG) that is so far out, dreamy, and inventive that you binge-watch episodes of the Shark Tank dreaming that you are on that show, pitching this wild idea. Stop fantasizing and start actively working on it. For some ladies, this is a tech start-up that will cure world hunger. For others, it's the newest gadget to make changing your baby clean and safe while out and about. And for others, it's about moving to an island and hitting a total reset on your life. Who does that? Well, I did.

And before you start exclaiming, "But, Dana! I just don't have enough time. I spend ALL of my time in the 60%."

First, read (or reread) chapters "D is for Delegate" and "H is for Help."

Then, do the following exercise.

You have 168 hours in a week. No amount of money or pleading or prayer is going to give you more.

168 hours. That's it.

Let's tally out how you spend those hours. And remember, answer these questions as honestly as you can. No one's going to judge you here.

In one week, how many hours do you spend:

- Sleeping?
- Working?
- Maintaining your household (think laundry, cooking, cleaning, etc.)?
- Attending kids' activities?
- Going out for date nights with your partner?
- Volunteering?
- Working out?
- Practicing general hygiene and self-care?
- Interacting with friends?
- Scrolling on your phone?

Add all your categories to this list. Now, tally up the hours you spend on these activities. If you're like me, your hours will total more than 168 the first time you do this. Do it again!

Now, go through those same criteria and add how you would *like* to spend those hours.

It probably looks wildly different than the first round. This is because most of us spend our time doing things we think we *should* be doing instead of the things that bring us joy or help us feel fulfilled at the end of the day.

Well, no more. Use that new list with your ideal hours as a blueprint to design your days, weeks, and months!

The Big So What?

No one can buy more time, not in a day, a week, a month, a year, or a lifetime. How will you spend each increment? Use this chapter over and over again to come back to yourself, what you really want and desire to continue exploring new ways to spend time with time.

F
is for Failing
– Not All Failures are Created Equal

*"You may encounter many defeats, but you must not be defeated.
In fact, it may be necessary to encounter the defeats,
so you can know who you are, what you can rise from,
how you can still come out of it."*
— Maya Angelou

Failure. A single word that hollows out a pit in our stomachs and breaks us out into a cold sweat.

Why are we so afraid of failure? Despite our intuitive knowledge that it is simply a part of life, we avoid it at all costs. There is failure, there will be failure, and we must embrace failure in order to grow. "Try" is one of my all-time favorite songs by Colbie Caillat. It doesn't matter what anyone else thinks. Doesn't matter if you fail.

Since you are reading this book, you are considering the terrifying possibility that I'm about to ask you to consider failing as a strategy. Well, I am. But before you decide I'm off my rocker, hear me out.

As women, we are made of so much more than we are given credit for. And more than we credit ourselves for, in truth. You know it, I know it. So, let's own it.

Let's start by looking at it through a new lens.

You watch a little girl with her mom from a nearby bench at the park. For the sake of this example, let's call her Ruby. Ruby is super excited to go down the slide. She's small and determined. Her mom is at the bottom, waiting to catch her. *Swoosh.* Down she goes and sticks the landing! Ten points. Ruby's mom catches her and embraces her with a "Great job, sweetie!" Of course, Ruby wants to go again. Off she runs to climb those little steps, mountain-sized in her eyes. And again, down she goes, but the slide is too fast this time.

Her mom is too slow. She can't catch her. Ruby spills off the slide onto the grass beneath. *Thump.*

Tears gush from Ruby's eyes. From total elation to complete meltdown in three seconds flat.

Mom runs over, frantic. What do I do? What can I do?

She picks Ruby up and dusts her off. And with a hug and voice that soothes skinned elbows and cures scabbed knees, she says, "You're okay. You were so close. Go again. You can do it. I believe in you."

And with a kiss on the cheek, Ruby is ready to try again. She sticks the landing. 10 points. A shower of hugs, kisses, and "Woohoos!" and the game begins anew.

Now, I'd like to say that I just told you a faithful account of how I handled a perfectly pleasant day at the park.

But that wouldn't be the truth.

When my oldest daughter was born, I was too new, too unsure, and too depressed to treat her failures in such a healthy manner. I really screwed this up. And would continue to screw it up for many years to come.

She's now 23, and, in truth, I am only just now getting it right. As is she. Together, we are building our failure tolerance muscles. And in absolute truth, there are times when she's better at it than I am. She's a Jiu-Jitsu fighter and, thus, an expert at falling and getting back up. Literally.

However, when she was young, around three or four, she was my precious little girl—my *first-born* baby girl. She seemed so fragile and risk-averse, and I played right into that. When she fell off that slide, I overdid it. I coddled her, cooed at her, and promised her that nothing and no one in life would ever hurt her ever again. I shudder now at how I reacted.

We all get hurt. We all fall down. We all choose a loser (or 20) to date. We are constantly facing opportunities to fail. Those of us who learn to embrace failure, fail fast, and get it over with, learn and grow so much faster than those around us who are terrified to fail. These are the most successful women in the world. Why? Because we have a tough ass. It doesn't hurt that bad when we fail. We understand that this is part of the growing pains in this game called life.

Now, take my second-born daughter, who is now 19. It's a totally different story, but it's the same slide. I was more equipped with mom knowledge and supportive friends who showed me that some pain for our beloved children is normal and healthy. I was ready. When she was flying off the BIG slide, she ended up on the grass. Did not stick the landing at all. 1 point. I helped her up, wiped her tears, and gave her a giant high-five. I said, "Good job! That was awesome. Let's go again!"

Today, she still takes herself less seriously than her older sister does. She is more inclined to take risks, albeit in a calculated way. Is she more open to failure and putting herself out there despite the great unknown because of that day on the slide? I doubt it. But I'll never know for sure, nor will you. So, won't you try failing? Join me. Tough asses are in!

So, let's learn how to fail, shall we?

First, there are Big Fs and Little fs in failure. Separate these before embarking on your journey of potential failure. The possibility of encountering a Big F failure is slim. Going bankrupt, having your start-up go under, leveraging all of your assets and worldly possessions to invest in a too-good-to-be-true internet marketing deal, you get it. The big, giant, terrifying, long, and hard-to-recover-from types of failures are rare, infrequent, and mostly unlikely.

Little fs are your everyday failures – the ones we avoid the most. They're the 10% stretch we're unwilling to take because we're comfortable where we are. Any deviation from the course might lead us astray.

But, of course, it might also bring us bigger, better horizons.

I am saying this as someone who sees women shy away from pushing the walls of their comfort zones almost daily. We are not playing enough to our strengths. We are not putting ourselves out there as much as we want to deep down inside of our souls. We are not promoting ourselves as fully as we are certainly capable of. We are afraid to fail.

In what ways are you currently set up to try new things at work? Are you offering to take on things that are a stretch for you? We're not talking about totally out of your comfort zone and expertise. Stretchy things, like a great pair of leggings, are forgiving and breathable.

Okay, smarty, how do I do it and not lose my critical day job?

Stop playing small. Play to your strengths instead, amplify your voice and your gifts, and share your wealth of wisdom with bravery and bravada in our hearts.

And no, I didn't spell it wrong, you grammar witches (big shout out to my editors; you are gods and goddesses amongst men!). I changed the word bravado to the feminine way I want to spell it in our honor going forward.

My secret spy name is Bravada. She was born as a phoenix out of the flame. She is a badass and not a bitch. She is making a huge difference in this world and is not burned out. She still has a lot left to do in this world, including every woman who wants to stretch to her full potential to get there. She is harmonious and joyful and bold.

She is Bravada.

We have to try, fail, fix, and try and fail repeatedly, adjusting and tweaking along the way. This applied learning turns into highly valuable knowledge and, eventually, wisdom. Nothing is better than a wise woman feeling her power and bringing other women along for the ride. Scream on the way down. And then climb right back up. You are Wonder Woman. What is your superpower? How have you harnessed it and shared it with the world? Why aren't you taking that scary step and doing it now? In front of everyone, not knowing if you will succeed? It's scary as hell. And it feels so good.

The Big So What?

We've learned from our mothers, aunties, and older sisters of our best friends that failure is simply not an option.

But the truth is, you have nothing to lose but fear.

When you design your life's experiments as trials, you expect tribulations, correct? I see you nodding. Yes, that's right. Experiments sound way less dangerous than attempting to fail on purpose. We need to play some mind tricks with ourselves when getting out of our own way. Women have no business taking that type of frivolous risk. We have too many tasks to do, including all that fucking invisible work. You know, like other people's dishes, like our husband's and kids' and friends of the kids that came for dinner, and they're 12 years old and totally capable of doing their own dishes, and you cooked the meal too! Oh, oh, oh, and now, you're going to run to the store at 9 p.m. because the 12-year-old, oops, forgot to tell you that tomorrow's fundraiser for Sierra Club is a carwash and they need buckets, soap, sponges, and would like sunscreen, but you're all out. NO! (See "Chapter N is for No" for more) Try a bold, with a tinge of failure risk associated experiment instead.

My dear friend went on strike from cooking. FOR ONE YEAR. Yup, her husband and her 12-year-old twins complained about all her cooking. She tried so hard to please them, making separate meals, which didn't work. Exhausted, she made one meal and said take it or leave it. Oh, they ate it, but complained. Then, those ungrateful people did it—they broke her last straw, so she set up an experiment. She said, "This week, if you complain and act this way and don't have serious attitude adjustments at the end of the week, I'm going on a one-year cooking strike."

And, you guessed it, they didn't take her seriously. She didn't believe she had the strength to stick with it, but you know what? She did! She made a sign and everything. After the year, she missed cooking a little, and, of course, they missed her cooking a lot! Today, I'm happy to report they got the message, and she stretched herself. She has helped many working moms design their own version of her strike approach. She didn't fail; she grew, and so did her family. And so will you, even when you fall. You will get back up and be better for it.

G

is for Gratitude

"The glass ceiling will go away when women help other women break through that ceiling."
—Indra Nooyi

And now, I need to share a *holy shit* moment with you all that happened to me. And why I'm so GRATEFUL that it did.

Many women have heard about, experienced, and even hit their heads until it bleeds on the proverbial glass ceiling. The first time it happened to me was at the tender age of 30. I was progressing in my corporate career and what is known today as "crushing it." Little did I know that the warnings were true.

If you ever find yourself climbing the corporate ladder and hyper-focusing on yourself and your own career, yet when you look around and next to you, and finally up—holy sea of white men, Batman! And, in my case, they were old—and mostly from Stanford. Cue ominous music.

The Ivy League comradery, golfing, yachting, and exotic dance clubs where these men "network" is no joke. Women simply can't compete in places where they aren't welcomed or sometimes allowed.

The tables are turning slowly. The Ivy League women I coach make their own tight circles and networks and create their own seats at the table. Take that, you dicks.

Now, it was in this scenario that my own limitation showed up.

Regardless, the other MAJOR thing that has to be explored here is another key G, Gratitude.

G is for gratitude, but not like that attitude of gratitude stuff that we've all heard over and over again until we cannot take any more attitude adjustments without ending up with a permanent attitude of anger-tude.

There are ways to make gratitude a daily practice that actually changes the way you feel situationally and relatively with the most positive hangover.

Here's what I mean.

Every single day, seven days a week, find time and make space. Create the habit of acknowledging five things that you're grateful for. Do it in the morning before your feet hit the floor or in the evening before you go to bed.

For those of you who pray, add it to your prayers every night. It's the perfect complement to what you're already doing.

For those of you who consider yourself spiritual, a little woo-woo, or simply open to the possibility that there's more to see than the naked eye in terms of universal principles, I strongly suggest that you put your gratitude practice into place before bed each and every night. It's just five things that you're grateful for. It doesn't have to be twenty-five.

And finally, for all the agnostics, atheists, and non-devout type readers, we love you too. Please find time once daily, whenever it suits you, to implement this practice.

Regardless of how you identify the easiest way to practice, make it simple, consistent, and routine, like brushing your teeth.

Here's how it's going to work for you every time so that you can count on it and get immediate benefits. Try it when you finish reading this chapter. You'll like it because this is an almost immediate joy producer.

First, say out loud the five things you're grateful for by counting on your fingers. That's right, you heard me. This is not a joke. I want you to count 1, 2, 3, 4, 5 on your fingers. It'll go like this:

One. I am grateful to breathe clean air.

Two. I am grateful that my teenage daughter smiled at me today, and it wasn't to get something she really wanted. It was simply a connection point with a real, genuine smile.

Three. I am grateful that I checked something off my list today that's dragged on for weeks. It's done now, and I can move on.

Four. I am grateful to my partner for making dinner tonight and doing the dishes. This was extra special because normally, we have an "if you cook, you don't clean" rule, and they did both.

Five. I am grateful that my best friend solved her own issue today and told me about it afterward.

The key to this type of gratitude practice is that no matter how long it takes (although ideally no more than five minutes), if you are super specific, as clear as you can be, and as articulate as you can muster, this will start producing joy immediately.

Why is it so important to be specific?

The more specific you are, the clearer you are, and the more articulate you are about the ways in which you're grateful, the more your brain and heart will recognize the type of gratitude you're practicing.

For example, are you practicing gratitude about yourself? Are you practicing gratitude for a loved one? Are you practicing gratitude for nature? The how is what matters, not the what.

Once practicing gratitude becomes routine, you will start to feel, notice, and experience the patterns of the gratitude elements that serve you best—the things that light you up the most and quickly bring you the most joy. And those are worth repeating.

Once you have a positive pattern established, you will start to rely upon your practice of gratitude to serve you each day, in every way, over and over and over, until you cannot imagine a day going by without finding five things to be grateful for.

Now, I know you are overachieving humans, but there is no extra credit for 6, 7, 8, 9, or 10 additional elements of gratitude. Simply do the five every day until you form your habit.

Before you move on to practicing your newfound gratitude tool, let's talk about some common excuses.

Sometimes, when teaching this joy-producing life skill, people tell me, "I just am not feeling it today." Or "I don't really have anything to be grateful for."

To be blunt, these excuses are bullshit. Most people I work with are incredibly fortunate, plentiful, and living a stable life without worrying whether they will be able to put dinner on the table or afford this month's rent. I mean, for goodness' sake. You have things to be grateful for; you're simply taking them for granted.

Start by being grateful for one thing. As small or insignificant as it may seem, other things will follow. It's a cold start problem that many people who are busy feeling sorry for themselves or hyper-focused on solving giant world issues have. They lose sight of the little things.

So, simply start with one thing to be grateful for and start yourself in an upward pattern.

Just in case you're still feeling skeptical or annoyed with me, I will help you problem-solve by giving you general jumpstart categories to think through when you're feeling stuck in gratitude. These are a few just to get you going:

- Friendships
- Pets
- Weather
- Flowers
- Acts of kindness done by you or that you have witnessed
- Family

The Big So What?

Have you ever heard the saying, "Be careful what you ask for because you just might get it?"

Be absolutely sure of what you want and why before you work yourself up into a feverish pace. For some of us, the drive to the top, where glass and cement ceilings exist, is an uphill battle THE ENTIRE TIME. If that's where you're at, take a minute to step back. Take a deep breath. Three deep breaths. In through the nose and hold for four counts, then out through the mouth and hold for four counts. Do it now. *"For women of color, there is no glass ceiling; it's way higher and harder to break through; it is cement."* –Nina Nelms, Nelms Music Planet (thank you for sharing this insight, my dear, dear friend)

Next, listen to yourself, the real you, that inner voice inside you saying, "WAIT A FUCKING MINUTE. NO WAY. I don't even want this climb." I Love Miley Cyrus and all that, but it's not always about the climb. So stop what you're doing and find a new way. There are more options at your fingertips than you realize. You can stay where you're at and accept that the role you're in right now may be good enough. You may even enjoy it when you're not having to scratch and claw your way to the top. It doesn't automatically mean that you're in a quitting situation. Perhaps you are good where you are, and your outside interests and passions will make up for whatever is missing in your life. You owe it to yourself to explore this as a possibility. Look for alternate routes, some of which may be a lateral move at the company you're at or even at another workplace with a better culture and work-life "balance" (their words, not mine).

So, let's say they offer reasonable working hours, clear expectations, are family-friendly, and embrace that you are an entire human beyond work with outside inspirations aspirations. And they don't stand in the way of that. Hell, they may even encourage it. Because they know that happy, fulfilled employees bring their whole-ass selves to work, and the more well-rounded they are outside of work, the more productive they actually are at work, too! What a concept.

If the answer is, "Hell to the yes! I've worked this hard for so long, and I need to know what it's like to make it to the top," then keep going for it. There's only one way for you to find out. No regrets, however, you need to get in the gratitude practice immediately. Acknowledge all that you already are, have accomplished, and will continue to accomplish for yourself, not just others.

H

is for Help – and Why We Suck at Asking for It

"Growing up, I always thought it was a sign of weakness to ask for help, but now I realize it's really a sign of strength to say, 'I need help, I can't do it all.'"

—Kerri Walsh

Alright, ladies, let's get real! We do not like asking for help. And when we do, we do it as a last resort and with a whole truckload of guilt (refer to "Chapter D is for Delegating" WITHOUT guilt). Why? Because you are a badass. You are strong and independent, and you can do it all, all on your own, all the time. And, really, only weak women would be callous enough to burden someone with an ask. You've been programmed and conditioned to believe this to your core.

So, let's dispel another bullshit societally inducted myth. When do we actually want help? This will differ for some of you, but generally, we want help with chores like, but absolutely and never limited to, washing dishes, laundry, cleaning toilets, or picking up avocados when we are making last-minute super-craved guacamole.

Now comes the tricky part. It may make you cringe a little, so prepare yourself. We NEED help when we are super sick and depleted from…? Sing it with me, "Burnout Baby Burnout!" No disco inferno. Only burnout.

We also need help when we are over-tasked, over-scheduled, and over-functioning. We know that we did it and do it to ourselves. We friggin' know. But we need our loved ones, partners and co-workers, employees, and cohort sisters to all be strong enough to tell us when enough is enough. Ladies, gather your group. The people you really love and trust. Look them in the eyes, and say, "TELL US!"

And then very quickly, within seconds, do something about it. Take something, anything, off your damn plate. It's overflowing. How do I know? Because you saw a book with "Burnout" on the cover and thought, "I probably need this." That's how.

You need to rely on the people in your life. And if they try telling you that you said you would take this on and this is your fault – if you made your bed lie in it – tell them to can their ego and help you in the same earnest way that you are asking for their help.

Look, whether we asked for this or not, here we are. We are in this trap that's called hyper-achievement. There is no distinction between work, home, out in our communities, etc. We simply are. So, your crew may as well get a clue (see what I did there?). They're going to help us.

Without this type of approach for help, we will burn out. And, when we burn out, all the way, it's not pretty at all. It's one of the biggest wastes of natural resource energy in the world, powered by high- and over-achieving women. See, if we don't ask and our network doesn't assertively (but NOT aggressively) offer to help us, we will extinguish ourselves. This may last one day, one week, or one month. Hell, it may last one year, like my friend I told you about who went on strike from cooking for her beloved yet completely ungrateful family. Or we may escalate to outsourcing in ways that they do not want!

What does that look like? Oh, I'll tell you. It sucks! For my family, that's no more Pozole with grilled cheese or quesadilla. And while we're at it, no more storing the old junk your kids left when they moved out. Oh, and no more using my miles for your upgrades. You're too privileged anyway, and I earned that shit. The list will go on and on forever because I dance circles around most average achievers in my life, and what do I have to show for it besides these giant bags under my eyes?

The Big So What?

You must ask for help strategically and occasionally before you're super depleted. It will not kill you; it will make you stronger. AND you need those who know you and love you and value you and rely on you the most at work, in your home, out in your community, and within your friend group, to offer you this type of help from an informed point of view. Let's start this today. Send them a copy of this book with this chapter earmarked and one of those puppy-eyes emojis. They will get it, and they will take action. It will have to start and end with you because I'm talking to you! Yes, I'm now your official sassy Aunty. And I am also speaking on your behalf since they are reading my words and sage advice. Use me, I'm here for you! I got you, Sistah. I am you!

I

is for Independence

"I am no bird; and no net ensnares me:
I am a free human being with an independent will."
—Charlotte Brontë, Jane Eyre

Why, oh why didn't I combine Chapters H and I? Is it too late? Since you're reading this right now, I guess it is. Okay, then, here goes nothing.

If you're digesting Chapter H, you may have a little heartburn, and in this chapter, I stands for Indigestion.

Just kidding.

I is for the root cause of your problem, suffering from the *I can't* or *I won't* ask for help syndrome.

I is for independence.

Let me try to be serious, if for one chapter only.

Independence is defined in various ways: autonomy, caring for yourself, financial stability, etc.

Independence is also freedom from being governed or ruled by another country. This may sound out of the blue until you move to a Hawaiian Island, in my case, Kauai, where the indigenous people still fight for sovereignty from the good ol' United States of America.

And, for my least favorite definition, independence is the state of wanting or being able to do things for yourself and make your own decisions without help or influence from others.

Let's redefine independence for our sisterhood, shall we? Not in some new age, "woo woo" way. Let's make this real for today and tomorrow and for future generations of women. Independence to me is having your own bank account, with private access to it, so that if you need to get out of a shitty relationship, you can without fearing for your livelihood. Always have a small and livable nest egg sitting there. You decide what's enough based on where you live and how you are willing to live.

Also, please, pretty (you're so pretty) please have access to transportation when you leave the house. I don't care whether it's your ride or you bum a ride, you must have access to safe and reliable transportation for when you need to get out. Come on, we have rideshare. Never let anyone drive you on the first date. You don't know whether you're going to find Prince Charming or the creature from the black lagoon. Give yourself a way out. Drive yourself to at least the first three dates. And while I'm on this roll, live by yourself or with total (but heavily screened) strangers for a minimum of one year in your life. This is the best way I know of to get a true taste of independence. This is when you really learn who you are, what you want, what you're willing to settle for, and what you absofriggenloutely will NOT settle for. (Check out my first book, *Stop Settling, Settle Smart*, on all the ways to settle (or not) and give up the balancing act.) And these are not the end all be all of independence-building. But they are all solid and will give you the perspective, risk tolerance, and confidence you need to redefine your own independence.

The Big So What?

You will now make age- and situationally-dependent choices on having what it takes to live the type of independence you desire. How long will it take, you ask? I don't know! I'm not you. You want a range? Picky, picky. Then... AS LONG AS IT TAKES. This is not something to compromise on. I gave three very healthy and attainable and sustainable ways to get a basis for independence that's simply a foundation. Look, we're like houses. Without a solid foundation, there are too many cracks and issues down the road. Have you ever heard that a house is just a house until it's a home? You want to be at home with yourself independently. Map a plan for yourself that includes at least your minimum viable needs. Figure out what they are and then prioritize getting these things into place for yourself. It's really nobody's business what they are, how you are setting them up, or why. But you need these. And, in our 20s, they are not the same things that we will most likely need as a foundation or even a cushion for our tired ass in our 50s. I'm there now, and the cushion is a couch!

J
is for Joy

"To be happy is a choice you make every day, every hour. And refining and renewing that state is a constant pursuit."
—Julia Roberts

Jumping with joy for this chapter, I am. No, I'm not Yoda; I just talk like him sometimes. Do or do not, there is no try, baby! Guess I'll do.

Joy is one of the most precious and underrated elements I've encountered in my life, at work, growing up, and today as a leader of leaders in my coaching practice. Every space I occupy as a human is wrought with unjoyful people. And, when I encounter joy in people, no matter the context, it has this incredible osmosis effect. I feel more joyful, too! Have you ever deeply considered measuring the joy in your life? If so, how do you even start to go about it?

You give it a rating! On a scale of 1-10, how joyful are you today? How joyful are you at work today? How joyful are you in your partnership, marriage, or dating life? How much joy do you bring to others whom you care for?

Let's rate your joy now!

Are you both giving and receiving joy? Or is it just joyful all around and one score? Up to you; it's your joy-filled life! Or not. Now that you understand the measure and method. Let's get started. Take a pulse on your joy. Let's only focus on you right now. Many, if not most, of you are givers, nurturers, and gatherers (and hunters, too. I get it.). Your score will most likely include the joy you bring to others and, therefore, impact your self-score on how joyful you really are. I've been testing this with my coaching clients for the past five years, and I'm here to tell you joy is the one thing that most high-achieving and overachieving women will trade off in place of their own productivity and the value that they bring to others, despite how little others value them, be it in terms of compensation, gratitude, or added benefits. Picture this: I was leading a group coaching workshop for women at a well-known tech company. Did they want me to teach them how to climb the corporate ladder and deal with all the male misogyny or work with a board of directors for the first time like I had to learn? No. Did they want me to talk to them about the top three ways to build their confidence? Nope, not that either. What about how to get noticed and promoted? Still not even close. They simply wanted more joy in their days, especially during their LONG workdays, across the globe.

Imagine these strong, smart, and powerful women attentive and hanging on my every word. Now, picture them in breakout groups via Zoom and me going to them, class after class, room to room, encouraging all the microjoy ways and habits to change their joy factors. Doesn't this sound fabulous? And what a generous and benevolent company they must work for, where culture counts and women's teams are empowered to grow, change, and develop with "soft skills" and emotional intelligence. The harps, they are a playin'. What? You smell a rat? You're right! I cannot fool you. You're too seasoned, and you must have watched Maya Rudolph in "Loot" on Apple TV (If not, you have to binge it!).

Now I know when companies want to "hire" me to lead their ladies on the joy topic because they are investing in soft skills, I should RUN! If I read one more article from "Harvard Business Review" or Wharton Business School's Adam Grant on work-life stuff, I'll lose my mind (sorry, Adam, but COME ON. Don't get me wrong, props on your 1MM listeners on your podcast. Hit me up, let's discuss and debate). When the budget from a major corporation comes from the higher-ups, most of whom are old white men (have to say it, no offense intended), and the culture of said company dictated by that same cast of characters is to work a minimum of 60 hours per week and be extremely available and accessible on a moment's notice. Hell, they are, etc. It's a strong signal that there will be no joy. No soup for you! No joy, it doesn't sell or develop software. Or does it? Happiness makes people more productive at work, according to the latest research from the University of Warwick.[2]

Imagine my sadness, the opposite of joy, after truly doing everything in my power to help these women. I wanted joy for them so badly that I made myself, well, sad! I literally gave them 15 options for building microjoy habits that stick. And you know what? None of them worked. Total failure. If you read Chapter F, you may agree that this one is worth a capital F! For Failure. Or, in their case, F is for Forget. Forget about joy at work, and now that will spill into what's left of life as moms, friends, and wives and sisters because you have no time and no joy. They were simply stuck inside a corporate structure that had no pliability in this way. The higher-ups wanted a quick fix or get them off my back approach to building joy. Do you understand how devastating that is?

Now what? What are their options?

---

[2] https://warwick.ac.uk/newsandevents/pressreleases/new_study_shows/

Option 1: As much as I'd like to give you 15 options and combinations and permutations of what to do, I will not. You MUST get out of that company, not your job. Do not post out or up to a different role or department, there will be no joy there, either. Do not lift and shift yourself inside this place. GET OUT. Do yourself a favor, do not lament about how hard it is to start over at your age, or tell me that the market is too tight for what you do, or that you live in a community with super high unemployment rates, so the competition is just too fierce. Just save it. I spent 30 years leading and strategizing in the world of staffing and recruitment. If you want to get out, you can. The best time to look is when you don't have to, so start looking. Use a recruiter or a search executive to represent you. If you're newer in your career, hello, LinkedIn! Or just DM me. I'll tell you exactly what to do.

Option 2: MOONLIGHT. That's right, you heard me. You know that dirty napkin from that bar six years ago when you drew your big idea onto said napkin? Well, dust her off! There is something there worth exploring. Search everything from start-up biz plans to funding resources for women and minority-owned businesses to coaches who have been there, done that. I'm on five boards! I am here to tell you women like us will help women like you. Why? Because we like money. I'm kidding. Well, not really. I *do* like money. But I don't do what I do at this point for the money. If I did, I would NEVER write a book, host a podcast, or offer group coaching for up-and-coming women at an affordable and accessible rate. Here's the thing about money. If you do what you love and love what you do, the money follows.

Up to a point, maybe you're like I was, you're a single mom with a lot of responsibility and financial baggage leftover from that same dude you broke up with three times already. And then, oh that's right, you went and married him. NOOOOOOOOOOOOOOOOOOOOOOOOO.

Too late.

Ladies, I've been there and done that, too. So, try this.

"Love yourself first, and everything else falls into line." —Lucille Ball. Amazingly true.

And now, back to your regularly scheduled chapter on Joy.

When you put yourself first, there is joy. The joy stems from self-love. And, when the time is right, and your beautiful little seedling of a side hustle comes to life, you will leave that crappy corporation with your head held high and so much grace. It will be joy-inducing for you and countless other women as they watch you walk out, mouths agape, with your true dignity and sense of self-worth intact. You just *earned* your way out. NOTE: not *deserved*—that's entitlement bullshit. You created it and earned it, and now you're going for it. That a way, gals!

Option 3. Okay, this one is a doozy and, for most of you, will not work because you won't actually do it. But keep reading if Options 1 and 2 are not your jam. In this option, you are officially committed to producing joy despite the bog of corporate slop you're wading through. You are the joy leader. When does this actually work? Seldom. Where I've coached it into working is very specific, so sharpen your ears and listen up. There have to be some countertactics at play here. Yes, it's a bit like espionage. Here is how you'll approach it.

First, you need to have some clout and power, be a boss of something and someone (meaning a team of women), or at least be what's known as an executive sponsor. Sorry, just threw up in my shoes a little. I hate this term; I was this in many companies, and it still turns my stomach. OMG, the lingo. Anyway, it's true, so let's deal with it. An executive sponsor (sometimes called project sponsor or senior responsible owner) is a role in project management, usually the senior member of the project board and often the chair. The project sponsor will be a senior executive in a corporation (often at or just below board level) who is responsible to the business for the success of the project. Thanks Wiki!

Second, you need to have female balls of steel. Stop laughing; I'm not joking. You are not allowed to let the jerks (male or female or them, this is a universal concept) step on you or over you or ever ever ever interrupt you in meetings or hallways or virtual breakout rooms or meetups or parties, EVER! If you allow other women you are representing to see you as not all that and a bag o' chips, it's over before it's begun. You have to display an air of confidence that's not cocky or bitchy or assholey—leave that to all the others who actually operate that way. This is quiet, unwavering confidence that, when tested, comes out with a giant WHACK. For ways to avoid being interrupted at work, please visit my website at danamahina.com and watch our free videos on boardroom bullshit.

Third, this is the final criteria in this longshot option. You are going to set up a little micro-world inside of the overlord world you normally work in. It is entirely possible, just hard, to have a mini culture of your own inside your insulted team or even the workstream you represent. It is certainly easier to pull this off when you are, in fact, the direct leader of a group of workers. You will shelter and protect them and bring more joy to yourself this way for sure. If not, I'm not suggesting starting a revolution or a coup; that seldom works. This isn't "Norma Rae" (greatest movie of all time for women), and you most likely are not working in a Union shop. If you are, thank you, and you are truly a badass and made of more than I am. You teach the class, and I'll be your student. Hit me up, seriously. I want to know you and learn your ninja ways. And you are mechanical. I didn't get that gene.

The Big So What?

Dana Mahina, you focused totally on work in this chapter. What if I don't give a shit about that? It's just a j-o-b and a paycheck, and I work to live. Okay, I see you! Right on. Let's address that now. SAME DEAL APPLIES. The concepts throughout this book are transferable. Obviously, you must adapt the advice and tools to your own very individual situation. Even when we are in the same female storms created by society, we are most likely in different boats, meaning it is impossible and somewhat rude, even arrogant, to say, "I can walk a day in your shoes." Nope, not true. I cannot and will not, no try, sorry, Yoda.

So, let's take a few adaptation examples to get you started right where you are. Story #1: You're a stay-at-home mom (big job, go girl) with three little kids under the age of 10 tugging at you, no paycheck, not a lot of thanks, decent spouse, fairly living your life without too much to complain about, so why bother? You already have so much more than many others. You're good. WAIT, what about joy? How do you create more of it, share it with your spouse and kids and the mother-in-law that's suddenly living with you due to her aging condition. GET OUT! Just kidding. Perhaps you want to moonlight. Before you get all up in arms that I just don't get it, I said it myself, you are full up on responsibilities in the home, and now there are more with the dear mom-in-law. What you didn't consider is that perhaps she loves your kids and your spouse and YOU. And she is strong enough and independent enough to help with dishes (while you research work-from-home jobs that are super part-time) or even watching the kids after school two days per week so that you have time to volunteer at the animal shelter, which brings you so much joy. It's two shifts per week at three hours a pop, plus your drive time, so seven hours per week of no one asking you for grilled cheese or math support. Dogs don't do math, or do they? I bet they'd love your grilled cheese.

And what about you who mentioned that you really don't care about the job, you need and receive the paycheck, and you leave the rest at work until the next day? Good for you! Your joy may be cultivated in more insulation or micro-culture building time for you, yourself, and yours. YOU and you alone may need 30 minutes to walk after work and before you jump into your role(s) at home three days per week, or perhaps you're more like me and love your pets. Try this. Create a subculture of meditation, no meditation required, by petting those pets each morning for 5-15 minutes before getting out of bed. Ease into your day. Wake up five minutes earlier if needed. CAUTION: when you need to pee, please do it. Then jump back into that warm bed and get your cuddle time on with those pets. It is a dopamine joy-producing high that seems to last most of the morning every day. We call it Christmas morning. Every day!

K
is for Kyndrness

(Yes, brilliant readers, we realize that this spelling is funky. There is great reason… read on and find out why)

"Clear communication is kind, unclear communication is unkind."

—Brené Brown

In order to do this chapter full and complete justice, I bring you a real-time interview with the one and only Betsy Barton.

Betsy began her career as an academic astrophysicist, studying the evolution of galaxies, before bringing her data science and technology skills to finance and e-commerce. After working at a hedge fund, leading data science teams, and believing that astrophysics, quantitative finance, and data science are just three forms of the same skill set, Betsy founded Infiniscape in 2020. She launched its flagship app, Kyndr, in 2022 to spark a revolution of kindness and authenticity in social media.

All this is to say that Betsy is one of the smartest and kindest people I know, and a dear friend.

She truly believes that we can make the online world inclusive and friendly – and is working her ass off to make it a reality. She is the epidemic of kindness, and so are you! It's inside each of us, and together, we will forge a new path to a kinder, and dare I say gentler and more graceful world. What we have to do is become aware of our Kryptonite and kill it with kindness. When we are plagued with the Kryptonite of others, our power is gone. And, many times, as women, we take on other's negative and sometimes toxic energy. We are so depleted and zapped of energy we are wading in the nastiness of others. Look, the superpowers of women come in many flavors. We are driven, gritty, shouldering of others, and intuitive—just to list a few. When we encounter people who bring us down, tell us that we aren't good enough, step over and interrupt us, let alone the gaslighting, POOF, the power to be our highest selves becomes extinguished.

Nothing lights our flame more than one simple word, act, or example of kindness. Take social media as an example. For all the trolling and binge consumption that occurs, there are plenty of us watching way more than cool ways to pour chocolate onto a protein-rich mousse made with Greek yogurt or cottage cheese, although this is temporarily satisfying both visually and, in our stomachs, I've tried it, Yum! PLEASE check out VetCrew. I watch this hubby and wife vets taking care of every kind of animal, large and small, throughout war-torn Ukraine, and my heart just bursts with compassion. Gratitude and uplifting stories are the antidote to most types of Kryptonite, especially our own. You know, we all have it. We are the two sides of the same coin, both light and occasionally dark. Equal opposites are here for a reason. They show us what it feels like to be joyful, as we know sorrow, even when we unintentionally cause it.

The fastest shortcut to feeling good, that dopamine hit of "more please," is all about kindness. Try it. Say something super kind to someone that you don't really jive with or even like. Find something kind to say anyway, dig deep, warrior princess, there is always something. Even if it's, "I like your glasses." And mean it. Don't be mean! Now, feel your energy getting a little lighter and brighter and go for two more rounds of instilling kindness in others and yourself. Look in the mirror and say, "Hey Queen, hair is looking shiny and flowy today, oh yeah," or "Hey BFF, that color rocks on you, really brings out your eyes which remind me of the bluest water, remember that time we swam in the ocean? What a great day that was!" And your entire self feels right back there in that water at that time when everything felt good. That's what kindness can do for you and others, too.

Enter, Betsy!

D*:* How was Kyndr born?

B: It has taken several forms over the years, stemming from something that we have long thought of as "the dome," immersing yourself in a place, space, and time that's for someone like me, who suffers from seasonal mood disorder, to go. We sought to build a physical dome with projection tech to help people connect with themselves and others to get relief from life's ails. Then, don don don… COVID hit. We tried a few pivots that failed and created Kyndr.

D: Why Kyndr?

B: Social media is toxic and polarizing and has changed the way that humans interact around the world, affecting mental health, interpersonal relationships, and politics. Self-esteem, the way we show up in the world, not leaving our homes, increased suicide rates, body dysmorphia, and something has to be done.

D: Where do you even start?

B: Well, social media done wrong is destroying the human race. We offer an alternative that uplifts, engages with authenticity, and encourages authentic, real connections with one another to try new things that involve positive uplifting without fake news.

D: Wow, this is a huge endeavor, and any wife, mother, sister, or friend that you (and me as a founding member) have encountered along this hard journey to provide an alternative to the toxic wasteland of today's social media agrees wholeheartedly that we need a change, NOW. So, how do the incredible yet burned-out readers of this book get involved in an impactful yet productive way?

B: I want you to find creators on Kyndr that you resonate with, join their communities on Kyndr, and be a part of the mission.

D: Speaking of missions, what is your mission?

B: So glad that you asked. Let me be exact, as this is our guiding star that comes up in every fundraising pitch, board meeting, and interview I'm on. Our mission is to transform social media for the well-being of all permanently.

D: Sounds like a moonshot. Is it?

B: It sure is. As in Astrophysicist. I eventually arrived at a style that focuses on the biggest world problems, even though they are hard to solve.

D: When did you realize that solving the social media toxic issue was something you wanted to spearhead?

B: Like many entrepreneurs, I fell into it. I gradually realized how bad the problem is and how critical the solution is.

D: So, what now?

B: We are hyper-focused on bringing the most positive creators we can find and support to build their followings, messages, and offerings into genuine communities in deep, meaningful ways.

D: Sounds like a true moonshot to me. Talk to us about the brand and why "Kyndr?"

B: We wanted the name to reflect the goal. With so much tech dominated by men, this platform is built by women with women in mind.

D: To get people to be simply and truly kinder to each other on social media. How do you make the shift?

B: We have studied this for many years and found that our focus is kind and positive influencers with established followings.

D: Tell us your vision for the Kyndr world in 3-5 years.

B: People will be more aware of the damage caused by today's social media and, in the future, will be engaged in activities online and offline that are empowered by uplifting and positive platforms such as Kyndr and others, which we welcome. Conversely, the tobacco of our generation has been spawned by the Mark Zuckerbergs and Elon Musks of the world and others who profit from ad dollars, which continues to cause massive health and welfare issues. They specifically get people hooked and drawn into negative and toxic conversations repeatedly where they make money while making users feel sick, and in many cases, they become sick. Women and the Black, Indigenous, and People of Color (BIPOC) communities are affected even more negatively because these platforms are not heavily moderated, let alone effectively. On our platform, moderation is clear up front that we do not tolerate crude behavior, trolls, or sexual behavior. Via our strict moderation tools along with a culture of kindness, our AI is learning how to look for these offending activities, which, again, is part of our mission and vision for the next generations to come.

D: What is toxic positivity, and why should we care?

B: We are encouraging healthy discourse and debate, not what's known as *toxic positivity*. Toxic positivity is when people are denied the chance to express anything real, and they have to pretend to like something or be positive, even when they don't feel that way or are hurt by others. We are not the thought police here. You can't come in with hateful speech; however, you are free to voice your opinions and beliefs with open and kind conversations as long as you uphold our pledge.

D: What is the Kyndr Pledge?

B: To be the transformative force that redefines social media by fostering genuine communities that uplift well-being, kindness, and meaningful human connection.

D: Now that our readers imagine and ideally are a part of the Kyndr communities, what is your biggest dream for them?

B: That women find their people on our app that allows you to be authentically yourselves in communities that serve your purpose and help you to grow and flourish. In the long run, you will be drawn to our alternative, uplifting product and leave behind the apps that caused many horrible problems.

D: Thank you for joining me in this critical chapter about ways to be kinder to ourselves, others, and the world.

B: Thank you for caring about this issue so much and being a part of the Kyndr mission.

The Big So What?

Betsy is a long-standing client, friend, and joint-venturer. She prefers "pet nerd!" Together, we have grown, adapted, and bonded over the moonshot she has created. We also, at times, feel like we are on the deck of a ship in massively turbulent waters mid-storm, yet, together, we are better. I am so grateful for her willingness to invest in women in all the ways she does today. In particular, the company she has started has a kinder culture that changes the way women's lives at work, at home, and for themselves are up leveled despite today's huge challenges. If you want to start your own business, reach out to Betsy. She will act as the sage friend who tells you the absolute truth, the good, the bad, the ugly, and the beautiful, while making you feel good about your willingness to put yourself, your moonshot, and your mission forward. She's done this for many women over the years that I've observed with my own two eyes and my growing heart, and she proves to me every day that our intuition is the key to our greatest successes. We must listen to it. Kyndr is the port in your storm. Join us.

L

is for Leadership
– The 5 DIYs of Being a Good Leader

*"If you're not a leader on the bench,
don't call yourself a leader on the field!"*
—Abby Wambach

Cue 1950's radio ad voice

Have you always wanted to be a successful and inspiring leader? Do you feel you have what it takes to raise others higher? Well, have I got just the thing for you! My easy DIY 5-step method will have you leading others in no time!

Okay, okay, I'll cut the shtick. As much as I would like to give you an easy recipe to become an "instant leader," there just isn't one. Becoming a successful leader takes time, heart, and a lot of trial and error.

There are, however, five areas that I have seen in all great leaders and companies. And if you and your company adhere to being strong in these five areas, you will become effective leaders and market makers and put yourself on the path to accelerated success.

1. AUTHENTICITY

Nowadays, everyone is talking about transparency. Transparent numbers, transparent culture, transparent leaders, I could go on.

Transparency without authenticity is flawed, contrived, and worst case, can be seen as a cover to hide behind. Let me give you an example. If you and your company share your quarterly numbers with your employees but you only share the top line and the bottom line, you've technically checked the boxes for being transparent. But it is the numbers in between and the market that give the top line and the bottom line any meaning. Without depth, the numbers are surface, confusing, and devoid of meaning to employees who do not deal with the numbers on a day-to-day basis. This can cause the employees to shut down and not care. I'm not saying share all your numbers without reservation, but give context and explanation about the numbers, why they are important, and how the goals can be achieved. If people connect to your numbers and feel they understand them, they will want to impact them. If, after you share your numbers, an employee approaches you privately and says they didn't understand the numbers, an authentic leader will encourage the employee to speak up next time and will seek out a way to communicate the answer company-wide.

2. FAILURE

I know failure is kind of a strange topic to talk about when discussing successful leaders. The truth is that every great leader has failed in one way or another. When I was still in the corporate world, I reached a time in my career where I felt stagnant. I wasn't progressing at the rate that I wanted to be. I talked to our CEO, and he told me that it was because I had not failed enough. He explained to me that there are two types of failures: little fs and big Fs. Little fs are throwing things against the wall to see if they will stick. It's failing quickly and pivoting fast. This makes little fs more like lessons. Examples of Big Fs are start-ups that fail, bankruptcy, or losing your top account when you have a lean portfolio. These types of failures are big, obviously, but also fuel a fire to go for the next big thing. Up until that point, my life was planned and designed. Even though I had tried some things that didn't work and had been rejected, I wasn't comfortable with little fs and was terrified of big Fs. I was scared to fail, but without failure, you cannot have success. Failure accelerates the need to succeed and provides lessons learned for future application.

3. FOCUS

Focus puts your vision on the things you actually need. Multi-tasking is the way of the world, but if you try to do everything, you will be mediocre. It's that simple. Focus ensures that you only put your time and energy into the things that really matter. You cannot have clarity without focus. This leads me to my next point…

4. CLARITY

Clarity is the most important part of a successful company. Clarity is the laser focus on what is already in your line of sight – clear, simple, objective. A successful leader will articulate this so everyone knows where they are headed. Clarity and focus must work together. In the last company I ran, we were stuck at a revenue number when I joined. To break through the barriers, we needed to diversify our portfolio and create products and services that were ancillary to what we do. We identified critical areas, and with authenticity, failure lessons learned, external viewpoints from clients and partners, and internal feedback from employees, we devised a four-point focus plan for the year. The four points were: grow revenue, contain costs, scale, and brand awareness. When we rolled it out, we did it with hyper-focused clarity. After the meeting, I told everyone that if they were asked to do anything that does not fall into these areas, come and see me to help them say no. That was the year we doubled the size of the company.

Clarity also applies on an individual level. No matter what type of person you are, I have found that having one north star is critical to success and motivation. Again, multi-tasking may be tempting, but don't confuse tactics with strategy. This applies throughout your life; promise yourself that you will take focus and clarity to the things that truly matter. If you are struggling to give up multi-tasking, I highly recommend reading "The One Thing" by Gary Keller. It will revolutionize your thinking. Market makers like Starbucks, Netflix, and Apple have one big-rock goal each and every year, known company-wide, and they are maniacal about making it happen.

5. RESULTS

One of my favorite sayings is, "Ideation without execution is hallucination." If you sit around with a bunch of great ideas in your head but never act, you are halfway to nowhere. Results are the measure of how well you do in all of the previous areas. The results that count are the ones that matter. I know a lot of people who get a lot done every day, but somehow, the important things are left on the backburner. You can be productive in the wrong way. What is important will vary from individual to individual. It's not about just doing things right; it's about doing the right things. Boards and executives that lock themselves away without looking up and out or getting into the guts of their business will have a hard time getting predictive results.

The Big So What?

Transformational growth comes from identifying the right things and then doing them right, all under the blanket of authenticity. This is a DIY project. You need to set goals for yourself and your company that concentrate on all five areas to transform yourself, your team, and your company into market-making leaders. And if you find yourself in need of a little DIY jump-start, try me!

M

is for Motivation
– Matching My Time with Your Effort

"Don't compromise yourself. You're all you've got."
— Janis Joplin

I have been putting off writing this chapter due to a lack of M. This is such a difficult topic, so the best way for me to unpack this is to get deep into your psyche and perform Jedi ninja mentalist tricks on you as only I can with my military level of intelligence on decoding humans. Or, to sum it up, ALL of us sometimes lack motivation.

I don't know why we procrastinate. I don't really care, and neither will you after reading this chapter. How about we shortcut the shit out of this topic?

There are literally thousands of therapists, apps, coaches, and counselors, all of whom acclaim that they have the secret to unlocking your full potential. Given that we all have access to answer just about anything at our fingertips or through voice-activated ChatGPT robotics, don't you think that's just silly? You don't need to know a secret. You need to get out of your own damn way. Period. The best way to do this is by taking a tiny, baby, teeny-weeny, micro, or nano step towards what you want, which you are currently demotivated to do. Easy, right? Maybe not. But it is simple. And, simple is your best lady in waiting. She is there whenever you need her, on the ready, any time, any place, and anywhere, so no notice or formal invitation on fancy paper. She is there, so it is best you use her. This book is the culmination of my life's best work, distilled down for women by this woman and designed for the ages of future women as timelessly as possible. I know some stuff about some stuff, for sure. What I don't know, I simply don't know, and that's okay. No one knows it all. Here's what I know above all else. When you take that step toward your goal, you are one step closer to having what you want, truly desire, or even need. Thanks, ladies, I'm here all night! My work here is done. I'll take my final bow.

I told you it was simple, just not easy. So, take that step. Do not judge how small it is or if it's right or wrong; it's progress and forward momentum into the future. It's getting yourself unstuck without a bunch of hoopla or complaining. Just step forward. Go towards that something. Now, let's see how motivated you are. Take writing a book, for example. NOT EASY, and for many of us, not simple either. And girl, we make it hard, then harder. We are such tough self-critics. OY!

As I'm working on this chapter, in real-time, picture me feeling that classic lack of motivation or self-doubt. I'll help another client or friend and avoid writing despite the deadline that I have to meet. Oh yeah, this is the real deal. I'm stuck in this writer's block rut. What about you? Is it a blog that you're avoiding? Or a paper for your dissertation or your super-secret romance closet writing that you've wanted to do for YEARS but are just not sure will work? What if you look like an idiot, or your recreation of the viral Christian Grey isn't hot at all; it's a steaming pile of boredom in the bedroom, so why even bother? As your antidote to burnout continues, bothering to try may mean the difference in creating energy, space, excitement, and opportunities for yourself vs. turning into EEYORE from "Winnie the Pooh."

Sticking with writing is an example to which you may relate, even a memo for work, a policy change, or an offer letter. Many of us would rather heavy lift our way to helping others like dear sweet Kanga instead of carving out a few minutes to get started on something we feel unmotivated to do. So, it's a real conundrum. If you are unmotivated due to burnout and said project will not bring you enough joy, energy, or satisfaction to be worth it, SKIP IT. Don't even start or try. It's a waste of your precious time.

On the other hand, if you really are that closet wannabe writer with a book inside of you that's dying to come out, you owe it to yourself to simply start and start simply. Write the title, one page, or an abstract of chapter titles. Just start. Then, you will know if the motivation that follows is an endless stream of consciousness, which, true story, happened while I was writing this chapter. I went from loathe to love in seconds as it flowed from my fingers onto my laptop via a split keyboard that allows me to type way longer without pain. Thanks to smart ergonomics!

The Big So What?

Just get going. Get off your ass and do a little somethin' something. It's the only way you'll know whether your issue or excuse really is due to a lack of motivation. Or, perhaps you have what's known as blank page syndrome or a cold start problem. There are so many ways in which we women stand still when this happens to us, bereft of options or even a basic understanding of what is happening to us. We are normally super busy, highly productive, and the go-to gals for everything and everyone. So, when lack of motivation rears its ugly head, it's a sign! Unfortunately, all the tarot cards and astrology will not get you into a motivated state because it's either due to burnout or avoidance of burnout, and quite possibly, you have good reason to be unmotivated, so honor that! And just don't do it, whatever it is. And if you are avoiding, avoidance is never a strategy. It solves nothing and is a clear indicator that, most likely, you just need to jump in a little bit, one toe in the freezing water, until you acclimate, and then a foot, and your leg, hey, you're swimming, and it feels gooooooooooooooooooooood.

Last quick tip in this chapter of M. Madams, there is this awesome and amazing tip I often give women who lead teams at work. And, lucky for us, it works in parenting, as Aunties and God moms, Big Sisters, and on that damn PTA committee where the other moms aren't pulling their weight. Here it is. Try it on whenever you like.

It's called, "Okay, fools. I will match my time with your effort. And that's it. Period! HAHA."

Here's a secret, we are more motivated than ever when we surround ourselves with capable, willing, able, and agreeable people who lift us up, take shit off our overburdened burned-out plates charred with soot from the countless times we've phoenixed our way out of the over-workloaded fires, and generally make life better at work and home and everywhere we go. And what do they get in return? You! And you're fabulous.

Finally, if you are wasting your precious time, effort, and energy on the people who are never going to get it, or truly contribute, or make it in their job, they don't deserve your time. Save it for those who deserve it, and together, you will always go further and faster, and that's so motivating!

N
is for NO – Practice Saying It

"Always remember: You have a right to say no without having to explain yourself. Be at peace with your decisions."
—Stephanie Lahart

The best way to get good at saying no is to practice saying it.

I'm serious. You need to start saying no.

I teach the three types of No—No. No? and NO! Do you see the difference between the three? Try saying them on your own first, in front of a mirror or your phone's camera. Come on, try it! Then, get a partner. On a day where you simply don't give a shit what anyone else thinks because, like me, you are now over 55, and this is it. The others don't count; it's all about what I think, believe, and feel now. Here, you will try it in a group, for example, at a dinner party, work event with your friggin LeanIN circle, or the park with the moms group. Once you achieve the harmony that comes from a resounding NO, you will never forget it and start channeling that shit! Can I get a "Hell NO!" HELL YES to that.

Often, you will find when you're trying to say no, you stand in your way. You can't seem to stop thinking about how you have to say yes or you're somehow letting other people down.

The BEST way to get out of your own way is to break your state. BREAK IT! Have you ever heard of the term "pattern interrupt?" Let's talk about the good ones and the ones that you do not want anymore, EVER!

A pattern interrupt is a technique to change a particular thought, behavior, or situation. Behavioral psychology and neurolinguistics programming use this technique to interrupt and change thought patterns and behaviors. Let's say you read this chapter on a Saturday morning, and your day and evening are free. Throw what you need MINIMALLY into the car and head west, east, or wherever. Just head out! Go explore and allow the wind to blow your hair and the road to take you on one less usually traveled, ALONE! We have to get you out of your head; it's scary in there!

According to the National Science Foundation, humans average up to 50,000 thoughts per day.[3] 50-freaking-thousand. Amazingly, about 95% are repeated thoughts. That's a lot of repetition. And very little space for new thinking. Einstein's theory, anyone? If you haven't heard it before, Einstein's definition of insanity is doing things the same way over and over again and expecting different results. Too much repetition makes us nuts! So, it's time to jump into the game of pattern interrupt.

Before I unpack the quick and simple ways to do this, I want to give you a jump start to spark you out of old ways and into new, healthy, fresh, and fun ways of living.

What is your zip code?

---

[3] https://magazine.wharton.upenn.edu/digital/the-impact-of-limiting-beliefs/

No, you didn't read that wrong. Answer the question. Write it down. Now!

Now, add all the numbers from your zip code in your head (No calculator! Pen and paper or fingers only).

Still stressing about all your repetitive thoughts? Didn't think so.

That's called a "break state." It's the jump start to your pattern interrupt. Basic mental math is hard for most of us because we don't do it in our everyday lives. Most of us, anyway. Therefore, your brain actually has to work on something it's not used to. It stops the repetitive voice in your head in favor of desperately trying to remember what 14 + 8 equals.

Use pattern interrupt and a break from whatever you're worried about, working on, or wondering about. Your brain deserves it.

Let's try another now that you're on a roll and getting the hang of it. Let's put the "Ahhhhhhhhhhhhhhh" in AHA! You get it. You really do! With gusto.

What was the last meal you cooked or a loved one cooked for you? (If you don't cook and no one around you cooks, what was the last meal you ordered for yourself at your favorite restaurant?)

Picture it, smell it, feel all the feels about that meal. MMMMMMMMM

Now, focus on one ingredient from that meal that stands out for you and your senses. You may choose a spice that's the winning factor. Let's say, for this example, you were eating curry, and the spice was cumin or turmeric. You get the point.

Next, describe those spices. Really get into it. Tell me about the color, taste, flavor, and degree of heat or lack thereof. Is it silky or smooth? What childhood memory is it sparking? Be with all that immersion state for a few minutes. Enjoy it!

Now, your brain is really thanking you and is up to tackle whatever you have planned next.

The break state tool can be used anytime, anywhere, any place for any reason. It's just right there and available to you and your team at work and loved ones at home. It works so well, and women really love the little respite from the incessant buzz of their over-planned and over-functioning lives. Feel free to reach me on social media for more ways to break out of the constant hum of your mind.

> "Say this prayer silently or out loud to yourself:
> I forgive my past, I release the future,
> and I honor how I feel in the present."
>
> —Gabrielle Bernstein

The best part of deploying these tools is that you will now make better and more informed decisions on when to say yes to stuff that you really want to do! And the things that don't bring you joy or help you be your most productive, amazing you, the things that drain your value and cause you to feel depleted and resentful, will flow naturally into your basket of NO.

And now, for the pièce de resistance, how to overcome your fear of public speaking by using a break state, in case you would like to do a TED Talk or speak at your local PTA event, meetup, or tradeshow. I taught this trick to my daughter and her classmates before they presented their pitches in design thinking at high school, to incredible public speakers with important messages to deliver, and to many strangers who were freaking out next to the alter at the wedding venue when it's their turn to make the toast. Seriously, this shit works! Take a rubber band and SNAP it on your wrist. Snap it real hard. OUCH, that hurts. Damn right, it does. You know what else it does? Gives your super anxious nervous system something to really focus on. Pain! And before you know it, you aren't stuttering or stammering or making excuses powered by profuse sweat down the butt crack of your silk chiffon dress that you simply cannot get up there and open your mouth. It's too dry, and you've forgotten your own wedding vows, and they aren't written down, and if they are, the cute little pink index cards with wedding bell graphics are shaking so profusely you cannot read the words written on them. You are punch drunk with worry, fear, uncertainty, and doubt. Fear of public speaking, or glossophobia, is estimated to affect 75 percent of adults, as recently reported on NBC World News.[4] And you know what's even more sobering? This causes women to say NO when they really mean or want to mean YES. When was the last time you considered giving a talk in front of peers at work or any audience? Did you end up referring another great gal pal to do it because she's a "better" speaker, expert, or more "qualified" than you? We second-guess ourselves, don't we? All the time! We do this when we lack confidence and face the crippling fear that we will freeze up at that podium or break into a visible sweat due to Mic Pack equipment that's taped to our skin under the damn Spanx we decided to wear to "look" our best. Why even bother speaking? Just say no or refer it out, right? Wrong! You can do this! Snap that rubber band or break an old school pencil, the No. 2 kind, behind your back right before you speak. It's harder than you

---

[4] https://sites.bu.edu/ombs/2017/11/27/what-is-glossophobia/

imagine. That pencil is behind your back, and you have to put in a lot of effort to break it. You'll see. And once you do, it's such a release. What a rush! Now, you're ready for anything. Go speak your heart out about your favorite topic du jour.

The Big So What?

If you take a page out of the most successful AND joyful women's playbooks, they say no ten times to every one yes. Why? No makes room for yes. I'm up to an average ratio of 5:1. Where are you at? Time to take the challenge? Join my women's group on social media, come onto the Kyndr platform, or wherever you find me on social and join the challenge. You can do this, we will do this together, we will learn to say No!

O
is for Opportunities – Created by Outsourcing

> *"Not knowing when the dawn will come,*
> *I open every door."*
>
> – Emily Dickinson

Planning your strategy in the corporate world for the immediate future and building on that for mid- and long-term is probably second nature to many of you. So, why have you, a high-achieving, successful, ass-kicking woman, not yet applied this talent to your personal life? Is it because you've been told not to boss your husbands around? Or do your kids tell you to turn the boss lady or (in my case) coaching off? Or worse, do you actually believe that we are not supposed to run our daily lives outside of work as if they are our businesses?

If we are totally strategic, accomplishing great stuff, and highly effective females at work, why not apply this wisdom at home? Shit, it works for the PTA, community projects, and church activities. It works everywhere we choose to show up because we have a strategy. We have a blueprint and a horizon plan for getting shit done. It *is* universal. How about all y'all stop being so goddamned threatened and embrace your baddass-ery? That's right, I am a sassy, badassy type of gal. That's just who I am! Deal with it. NO! Wait. Better yet, learn from it and help me!

When I ask for help, which we all know I mostly suck at, it's most likely because all my heavy lifting, smart approaches, and a plate of stuff is simply TOO MUCH FOR ME. I ask as a last resort and when I really need it. The more I'm met with resistance, whining, and sheer and total lack of effort, the harder it is for me to ask again. Cue the "bitch," and the vicious cycle continues.

Because I do need help! I **need** it. We all do.

I give you this next piece of advice in the full knowledge that I SUCK at it. But I need to get better. And so do you! So, instead of allowing ourselves to be discouraged and eventually "bitchy," ask for help early and often. Get others used to it. And be very savvy in your asking. Use your beautiful head on those shoulders and ask people who want to support you and will try their best to do so, especially when you can play to their interests or strengths.

Now we're cooking!

Next, let's take a business concept that is super helpful, truthful, and eye-opening and apply it to your life! It's called the SWOT. You've probably heard of or used it before.

SWOT asks, "What are the Strengths, Weaknesses, Opportunities, and Threats happening in/to my company right now?"

When you work on this type of framework, it doesn't happen alone in a vacuum. It's a collaborative and highly effective tool. Did you know that many consultants charge big bucks to ask you thousands of questions and create the output in a SWOT map? Not today, my women. Today, we are going to make this simple, practical, and actionable. Let's dive in and look for the opportunities that exist for you right here and now.

I want you to block time in your already jam-packed calendar. Yeah, I know. Spare me the excuses and do it right now.

Block time for four sessions with an accountability partner, 30 minutes per session. Go ahead and set a timer so that you don't go over. If you finish early, excellent! Take a walk or meditate with the extra time.

Session 1 is all about your Strengths. List them ALL. Brag about yourself! If you don't, no one will. You will not embellish. I promise you. We're women! Most of us wouldn't know how to brag properly if our lives depended on it. Go for it with gusto and use your key accomplishments in life, not just at work, to make this list.

Session 2 is all about your Weaknesses. DO NOT BE MEAN TO YOU. This session is not meant to undo all your good work in session 1. List the things you really struggle with and use **kind** language. Pretend you're talking to a friend about their weaknesses. If you're indecisive or fearful of tough decision-making, these all count. Notice how I word these things. We all suck at something. We are human, after all.

Session 3 is all about Opportunities (and what this chapter is about). What opportunities are available to you right now? To help you get crafty, have your accountability partner ask open-ended questions like: Who is offering to assist you right now with legit help? Perhaps it's resume writing or babysitting. What promotions are posted at work that you've been too self-critical to apply for? These are still opportunities. You may not want to apply for them, but you should list them anyway. Go ahead, write them down. This is for your eyes only!

Session 4 is all about Threats. What threats do you face to your goals or the opportunities you listed? Now, for the difficult part. Are these threats real, imagined, or mostly worries, preoccupation, and fear? According to psychologists, 99% of the crap we worry about never comes true. Once you've got the 1% of actual threats, rank them. Are they threats in your way now or coming around the corner? Get it out of your head, heart, and stomach and onto your list.

Now, take inventory. Are you maximizing your strengths to offset your weaknesses? Are you taking decent and calculated risks to ward off threats?

Are you outsourcing? Why is outsourcing so important for today's crazy-busy, overscheduled, and often underpaid women? SURVIVAL.

The Big So What?

Look, if you are not the dish queen or a fabulous (or even decent like me) cook, or worse, the mere thought of cleaning your toilet bowl makes you gag, then, lucky for you, outsourcing is available right now! There is nothing, I mean absolutely nada, wrong with looking at what you love and what you loathe, and for the loathing category, outsource that stuff. You can't afford not to! Yes, yes, I tricked you. I didn't say you can afford to. And don't forget to share your newfound ahhhhhhhhh with us at danamahina.com! You may earn a prize. No, really, we send stuff out as rewarding reinforcement. I told you; I got you!!!

P
is for Productivity

Being busy and being productive are not necessarily the same.
Many people keep busy to avoid taking action
on things they're afraid to pursue.
— Lauren Mackler

How often have you noticed that being busy, super busy, is not the same thing as being productive? There is a reason for this. Our efforts are not measured by the pound but rather by the punch they make. Truly, dear sisters, your worth is measured in the impact you make, not the grey hairs you accumulate with sweat.

I have so many stories here to share. Let me start with a team I was managing over a decade ago. These were smart people, VERY smart people. If you like the show "Billions" on Showtime, you will understand my Wendy to their quant pod (a pod using a group of three or four brilliant analysts on a team to crunch the numbers, trend the data, and predict things). If this sounds like a foreign language, let me explain. On "Billions," Wendy is the performance coach working inside this super disgusting and unscrupulous hedge fund. Her job is to make people inside the company optimal. Sometimes, she has to tear them down to build them back up so they can get out of their own heads and way and make gobs of money for their clients, themselves, and the fund. It's so juicy to watch, yet deplorable. Many times, the traders are easy; it's the quant team who need her uncanny ability to read people, get into what makes them tick, and find their Achilles heel and expose it. After all this "session" time in her private office with dark shades, they lay all their worries and crap on her, and she rewires them to be optimal. Boom. They are good to go make that money.

In reality, there are coaches like this, including yours truly. The difference is that coaches like me are helping you discover what's already great about you and how to make yourself even greater. When you're stuck or in a blind spot area at work (or home, wherever), we show you where and why you are stuck there and what's happening around you to keep you stuck. The most gratifying part of what a performance coach does is help you with options, angles, and alternatives. You see, we use all the tools in our kit to help you accelerate your own transformation. We never do it for you. We never intentionally cause you pain. Although, some growth can be painful. We help you uncover what's hidden or blurry; we bring things into plain sight so that you are more productive. Working with great leaders and aspiring ones, for me, has been a lifelong learning journey. The more I teach, the more I learn, and vice versa. In fact, the best coaches say that we teach what we most need to learn. And we do, and then we pass it on. When incredible women harness what they rock at and dump what they don't (or delegate it), the results become more and more productive and joyful, and then, the value given and received becomes a two-way street. Capiche?

Now, there is one more critical tool that I want you to practice. Practice, practice, practice. No, you will not be perfect; there is no such thing in human terms. Yes, you will become masterful at this. It's called the 3 Ps. They stand for Pithy (keep it short girl, land the plane), Powerful (pack that punch, that's right, go for the gusto and get to the exact target on the bullseye, that's the way, now you have their attention), and finally, Precise (clarity is everything, don't talk around things get to exactly the point you are trying to make and always remember, what is in it for them! Not you! Whomever the thems are.) Remember that old saying "WIIFM?" That is, "What's in it for me?" I'm suggesting start with what's in it for them. You'll get yours soon, in the form of JPV (joy, productivity, and dual-sided value) Hell yeah, that feels so good, doesn't it? Here's how I learned it, and now you will, too.

I worked for a female President of a Fortune 500 company when I was 32 years old and pregnant with my first daughter. Actually, I worked for the VP of Operations, who worked for the President. The President had a known propensity to make rapid decisions. My VP coached me and said that if I make a solid business case, hyper focus on what the company needs and how I plan to get there, I will be sure to gain her confidence and approval for what I was asking for. What she didn't tell me until the same day was that I would have two minutes or less to plead my case. WTF!

Good news, I was prepared, maybe overly so. I had a few slides and my pitch ready to go. I was nervous, so I practiced with my boss and at home with a friend with business savviness. I know I tend to overtalk when nervous, and I didn't want to start sweating profusely, so not a good day to wear silk, you feel me?

Okay, adjustment time. That same day, I knew the clock was ticking, within a few short hours, I'd have my day in the sun for two whole minutes. Vegas odds? I'd get a yes or no, she's decisive and has the power to make her own clear decisions, so I went for it. I got that ask down to a little less than two minutes. You bet I timed it… practice, practice, practice.

So, what happened? Did I nail it? Did I get a yes or did I get a no? I got a YES! More importantly, I learned a vital way to navigate and now hundreds of people, women in particular, have learned these three Ps as well. These lead to incredible levels of productivity by amplifying workloads into what really counts, and you will start to learn why busy work has to stop.

Try it for yourself. How many things on your plate (or platter) are busy work? In other words, you treat these things as critical, important, and urgent, when the three Ps will slash and burn these into perspective, and you can now start taking things OFF your overloaded schedule and calendar. You will start to slash and burn that stuff at work and home and out in the world, even at the gym, in exchange for what really counts and makes an impact for others and now it's your turn, for YOU! Now, it's about you! Feel that love.

The Big So What?

It is challenging for us to trade off being busy for productivity. I know that it feels weird and occasionally counter-productive. Believe me, you are so wrong. No offense intended. I know firsthand, and I've made this mistake and will never get those thousands of burned hours back. So, let's make you optimal right now. The best way to interact with others, whether peers or bosses, teachers or neighbors, is to be Pithy, Powerful, and Precise. Don't waste their time or yours. And whenever you're able, deploy this strategy. Go for the highest good, the highest impact, and the highest rewards within your reach when planning what to do and work on. One more, and you are there. That's a lot of ands. AND whatever you are thinking about taking on, if the effort required is high, it's a heavy-lifting, time-consuming, and resource-dense approach with little return on your time, effort, or energy, STOP. Don't do it. Without enough return, why would you do it? That's not valuing yourself now, is it? What advice would you give your kid? Or closest friend? You'd tell them to dump and run ASAP. Cause you ain't got time for that. We've all heard about ROI—Return on Investment. Let me stretch your brain a little. Now, I want to consider your Return on Energy (ROE) and, finally, your Return on Time (ROT). Otherwise, you'll find that it stinks, and that's why it's called ROT. Word!

Q

is For Questions
– The Killer of Assumptions
and Teacher of Root Cause

"Wisdom Begins in Wonder."

—Socrates

When I was little, I loved the show "The Odd Couple." Some of you will remember it.

Two grown(ish) men living together. One is very neat, clean, and organized, with possible hints of OCD. The other is a total slob, drinker, cigar smoker, gambler, and fun. In one particular episode I remember, the odds of their roommate-ship came to a head. They were constantly fighting and missing each other in terms of communication and ways to live together more harmoniously.

The buttoned-up guy, Felix, took out a giant easel and white papers, and the other guy, Oscar, sat in school-like wonder at what crazy tightly wound antics would be today's attempt by anal-retentive Felix to improve their living situation. In total exasperated frustration, Felix takes his black marker and, feverishly, while explaining the issues they have, scribbles down the word ASSUME. Oscar is still watching, almost waiting for Felix to fall on the ground in an adult temper tantrum for entertainment. Yet, there is a lesson and a learning and a major punchline to Felix's teaching. He says, "The problem with assumptions," now he circles the first three letters of the word, "is that they make an ASS of U and ME." Get it? They make an ass of you and me – ASS u me. And they do!!!!

I was very young when I watched that, and I'm sure my fuzzy, over-50 brain is not recalling the exact scene; however, it stuck with me.

In fact, you WANT to be curious about people, who they are, where they come from, what they do, and why and how they operate. This works on the internal levels, too. If we stay in open and curious places about ourselves and others, we simply stay neutral. This is an awesome way to avoid the dreaded judgment of others and ourselves that causes so much pain, negativity, doubt, and worry. There is one way to get into curiosity that works every time: a money-back guarantee. The sad thing is that unless you are a nerdy kid from the 70s like me who watches sitcoms and connects dots throughout life, or you are a lawyer or have legal training, you haven't learned the art of Socratic questions. As leaders, mothers, friends, sisters, Aunties, and mentors, all the other roles we women play in life are too many to count, right? This is the one foolproof way (even when we aren't acting as our best selves; we all have shitty days) to stay open and connect with others and ourselves in insightful and meaningful ways that cut through noise and red tape and save our energy for the good stuff. Once you practice these enough, you will find that they energize you and the other(s) if you aren't asking these questions only of yourself. These work universally, whether alone, one-on-one, or in a group.

Everything you need to know about asking excellent Socratic questions, simply and effectively may be found on kindergarteners' birthday invites. You know the ones! That's right. Don't overcomplicate this, and don't make any assumptions. STOP. You're doing it right now. Dana, it can't be that easy. Dana, it takes years to unlearn how I question things. Dana,

I'm not a naturally curious person. These are all assumptions, and what did we just learn? They make an ass of you and me. Leave the assholeing to the assholes; we are not those women.

Think about the last time you sent out, received, or saw a child's birthday invitation on someone's fridge. All the critical details, not too much and not too little, were listed on that invite, and they are usually quite small and follow the same format. This has been true for 50 years or more, even when they are sent out digitally with cute graphics. There is good reason. Imagine you send out this cute invite to any party and forget to list when it starts and ends. Won't your phone blow up? Everyone you send it to will email, call, and text until they know that vital detail that you forget to put down. Right? And then, you are so annoyed with yourself for forgetting. Before you know it, you resent the extra work of answering the same questions over and over again until you correct things by resending a blast email or text to all saying, "OOPS, the party starts at 6 p.m. and ends around 9 p.m." By using Socratics, we avoid assumptions and ensure that we don't cause others to either make them or cause extra work for our already overworked selves. Let's go.

1. WHO
2. WHAT
3. WHERE
4. WHEN
5. WHY
6. HOW

These starter words will set you free. Once you have all the answers that these entail, you will KNOW what the others are thinking and feeling and where they are coming from. You will drive yourself way less batty by applying these questions when contemplating your next move at home or what to make for dinner. The point is to avoid turning yourself into an intake system robot like the horrible ones on the phone prompts. Press "1" to book a reservation and press "2" to eject yourself from this queue forever because this voiceover robot is pissing you off so badly, fuck it. Free yourself to check yourself (and others) before you wreck yourself (and others). We simply don't have enough facts to make good decisions when we make assumptions. And we are usually unduly hard on others and ourselves when there are missing details.

Why not channel your inner two-year-old and ask why, why, and then why some more? The difference is that you are not a kid. You are a grown-ass woman. You are working on lessening your load and burdens, and this is the fastest and simplest way to do so.

Here's a great example. You work with someone who seems to take off every Friday at 3 p.m. The rest of you are still at it, punching that clock until 5 p.m. What the hell? She must have Friday-itis. How does she get special privileges? Who died and made her queen? And the boss never says anything while we pick up her slack. She must have pictures or something. Down, down, down the drain of jealousy and poor me places you go. Now, you and your other chickadee coworkers are bitching about her in the loo, that's right, the ladies' room. She walks in to pee, dead silence ensues, and she knows you're talking shit about her. And you all feel bad. What could be worse?

Instead, you sit down as a team with her (and ideally the boss) and ASK. Why does Judy get to leave on Fridays at 3 p.m. and we don't? How was this decision made? What are the parameters for us to have this same option? And so on. When you enter into these discussions, they are just that, discussions. There is no need for negative tones, assumptive thoughts, or an unwillingness to hear the actual answers.

Since this is a true story about a client of mine, I'll tell you what happened once I coached her to sit the crew down and explain where she was coming from. It turns out that Judy has a special needs kid. She needed to leave early on Fridays to get them to speech or occupational therapy. Judy and her boss made this deal when she was hired and worked out a flexible schedule to allow this due to unique circumstances. She is a team player who pulls her weight and then some, frankly. The issue was that neither Judy nor the boss ever told the team, and the team never asked. Assumptions galore and all around, up, down, and side to side. This is very bad. A little bit of Socratics goes a long way.

My client did not want to appear as if she was getting extra privileges or handouts because of her child. Yet, by not sharing a little, major assumptions were made, and hostility grew. She didn't want to share the details of her child's developmental disability with others in a new work environment. And, of course, that's totally up to her. But she missed the middle of the road where some information, like the essential details on an invitation, keep the gossip and judgments at bay.

I'm happy to announce that today, she has an amazing co-working relationship with those women at work, some of whom have become friends and met her child. You can never have enough Aunties on hand. It takes a friggin' village. Interestingly, she is also the boss now!

The Big So What?

How often have you realized there has to be a better way to approach someone or handle a difficult situation? Underneath that lies the simplest way I know how to teach women to lead. Great leaders help ordinary people do extraordinary things. Let's face it: only our ego tells us how special and amazing and superwoman we are. And it's only that same ego that drives up to be superwoman-like all the time, which is exhausting. We are humans. We have flaws. We are doing the best we can with what we've got. What makes us great and, even at times, extraordinary is being understood. The key to understanding is curious questioning powered by the insights of the Socratics. By simply asking who, what, where, why, when, and how, we learn so much about others and ourselves, and vice versa. The loop this openness creates is like a Celtic knot, never-ending and intertwining, no matter where it starts and where it completes; it's an endless loving loop of collaboration. I deploy this tool in my marriage (carefully, so as not to put him on the witness stand, "Where were you after work that took two hours and why are you so late?" etc.) Instead, I stay as curious as possible about what might he do after work. How does he like to spend his downtime after a hard day, and when he doesn't come home right away, is there a good reason? (Most likely the honey-do list I have waiting for him.)

R

is for Reality – Fact vs. Fiction

*"When women are "playing by the rules" in a rigged game,
it's time to change the rules. Break the rules.
Make new rules. Win the game!"*

—Erin Gallagher

That's right, we waste so much emotional, precious head and heart space day after day after day on things that are absolutely and unequivocally simply not true. My favorite client story is, I love you, B, and I know that you will read this and get all nostalgic about one of our first leadership development lessons we were working on where you said, "You told me not to feel anything." We had such a good belly laugh. I said, "NO! I told you to feel all the feels in the world, as long as the feelings are based on facts, not fiction." You went on to win a "40 Under 40" award and achieve so many other accomplishments. Proud of you, sister. Keep crusading!

There are ways to come up with solutions and answers strategically and effectively to problems at your fingertips and disposal most of the time. The issue is not that you aren't creative or resourceful. You're a woman! Of course, you are. You can bring home the turkey bacon and air fry it.

The critical issue is that when you solve for stuff and do it without all the facts, you are wasting your time, effort, and energy. What makes it worse? Wasting the time, effort, and energy of other high-achieving and overworked women in the process. Oops, and now they're doing it, too. Before you know it, smoke is coming out of your ears and curses coming out of your mouth. The air so thick in the room that even virtual workspaces can see a haze. In this context, you don't have all the facts or even enough of them to make good decisions. You're not making good choices or offering good recommendations either, are you? No, you are not. Why? Ok, you get it. So, what do you do?

First, step back, way back, away from that ledge. Next, gather all the facts possible to make a healthy and informed decision about whatever you are dealing with at work or home, wherever you are.

The issue is that many people will bring you things that are simply not true. Tales of fiction, even folklore, but despite how moving the story is, they are not worth factoring into the solving you will do. This will not work for you or anyone else either. You are a very smart and capable person; you are a woman. It's time to wake up and smell the fabrication and drama. And it's time to say STOP. I am not going to fall for your gossip dumpster fire about your coworker, little sister, or volunteer group. Listen, when people you interact with in all walks of life bring you troubles, unless you are a therapist, and Lord knows that I am not, this is a red flag.

Now, let's flip this same script to work. Let's say that you go to your boss, almost daily, with tales of woe about not having a seat at the table. You're never invited to key meetings. You KNOW that you're the topic of ridicule on email chains that go around the office and people hide their screens from you the second you walk by. Are these facts? Or are they fiction?

This was my great girlfriend/CEO, dealing with insecure, immature, non-productive, yet somehow always busy workers in her last gig, both guys and gals. She was the boss, and she acted like one. She went into discovery mode. She went on a fact-finding mission.

She talked with all the alleged offenders and offended and got to the bottom of the whining. 95% of it was not true, not even a little, other than the fact that people would minimize, not hide, their screens quite often, and do you know why? Their cube walls were short, and they were working on proprietary things involving HR-related issues and employees' payroll! Sheesh, they did this universally when anyone walked by too close to their screens. It was a habit, and a good one at that.

Once Madam CEO got all the facts, she was able to bring people in, one by one, and then ultimately, as a group, once she had made the rounds. She was playing with a very full deck and still is today, I assure you. She made it very clear to everyone involved and affected that she only deals in facts. And the best way to work with her and have a positive and supportive workplace culture is to do the same. From then on, the place became happier and more productive. The few women who felt ostracized, picked on, and singled out learned that they were wrong. They had wasted precious time, including the CEOs, unintentionally, of course. They are great ladies, just misinformed and running away with their stories of woe. And sadly, it took time and energy away from the accused offenders, who had NO idea why they were upset in the first place. To close out this case study, these women were likable and had a lot of potential to grow in their careers. One made it, and one did not. One stayed and learned to navigate with facts, not fiction, and have all kinds of feelings about facts, especially, when her counterpart quit, burned the bridge (never a good idea), and to this day, talks crap about the company.

Now, after digesting all of this, aren't you asking yourself why the woman who stayed, grew, and is thriving remained in contact with the negative? We are somehow drawn to drama and controversy. Stand firm and get away from it as fast as you possibly can. Don't be into it or them.

The Big So What?

If you were to add up all the wasted time you've spent on problems that don't exist and people that are simply not worth it, you would be sick! It's hundreds of hours in a lifetime, maybe more for us fixer/pleaser types. STOP IT. Get the facts, just the facts, and ONLY the facts clearly before you assess what to do. This is a universal tool from the magical bag of tricks—no magic required. When you know what's happening, your brain is excellent at clear and cool-headed decision-making. You may feel sad because you have to fire someone who is lovely but incapable of doing the job that they oversold themselves into or tried and tried and just find themselves in over their head. You may be super frustrated because you wanted them to make it and spent a lot of your own time and effort sharing expertise, cheerleading them, and still, nada. They don't have what it takes, and you hired them!? Look, there is an amazing leadership approach that says, "I will match my time with your effort." —Mary Kay Ash (later studied at famous business schools like Harvard)

And it's true! You want to spend the most quality time with the people at work and outside of work, where they are putting in their best efforts, vs. dragging along those that suck. However, there are exceptions to rules; in this case, the exception is that some people will not make it at their job. Some people will not make it in a marriage. And some people will not make it in motherhood. You gotta know when to hold 'em, fold 'em, and walk away. Time is the most precious gift, and it's not that long of a life. By using facts to have quality feelings, you will save yourself years of agony and help others, too.

Not to bring this into a dark space, but I feel it fitting to close this chapter with a sad yet revelatory story. My sister passed away when she was 25. I didn't say "only" 25. I am not bitter or avoidant. She lived a huge life in her 25 years. She was so clear with me that I was not to feel sorry for her or wallow in my grief for too long. She packed many lifetimes into this one, and she had no regrets. How many of us can say that at any age? 43, 50, 75, or older? Can you say that? If you cannot, it's time to start fact-checking and spending your time on what counts with those who not only deserve it but those who have earned it. I walked away from grief 35 years ago. Of course, I miss Jodi. Yes, it sucks sometimes that she didn't meet my daughters or my second and final husband. (Blessing in disguise that she didn't meet my "wasband." Whew. Dodged that bullet.) She was a tough and truth-telling critical can I get a hell yeah!? The facts are that it is sad and a bit lonely at times, and her life was designed by her and her alone to be exactly what it was, despite the illnesses and disability that got in her way. She was mostly fearless and went for it, whatever it was. And she got what she wanted in life. She wasn't taking no for an answer. Her secret weapons were logic, humor, and self-deprecation. What are yours? Deploy them now and always.

S
is for Self-love

You can be whatever size you are, and you can be beautiful both inside and out. We're always told what's beautiful and what's not, and that's not right.
—Serena Williams

When it comes to self-love, who is the worst at practicing it? That's right, W-O-M-E-N. Maybe it's time to recognize the men in all of us wo-men.

I mean, think about this for a minute. Isn't it the male energy and nature inside each of us that teaches us about self-care and putting our own needs first? Yet, do we listen to this part of ourselves that's as old as human time itself? No, we do not. Even when we are boss ladies and single moms, leading all day at work, at home, and out in the community. We simply do not practice enough self-care the way most men do. And where does self-love come from? Correct, self-care. Why is it so hard to love ourselves anyway?

Let's go back, way back. Let's talk about our bodies for starters, just rip the Band-Aid right off. In the time of the Rubenesque period from the 19th century, women's bodies that were curvy, soft, and voluptuous were heralded not only as beautiful but also rich! Imagine the times of hunger and famine and plagues, where anything but a feminine body that was sumptuous was anything other than desired. Look at the artists who painted these gorgeous creatures. Haven't you seen these paintings in any classic museum and thought to yourself, what happened to us? How did we get so obsessed with our bodies and, in particular, the notion of being fit, then thin, then skinny, and now worse, social-media skinny?

And this is only the tip of the iceberg. There has always been an ideal woman's body in every era over all these years. It used to be curvy. Now it is skinny. When curvy, soft, and voluptuous bodies were considered the beautiful female forms, naturally skinny women were declared underfed and twiggy. Now that skinnier bodies or bodies that are curvy in a **very** specific way are considered beautiful, women with fuller and more sumptuous bodies are considered unhealthy.

And who does this benefit? The billion-dollar beauty industry that thrives on women hating themselves. And who has the control? The men in power who get to deem women beautiful (read: sexually appealing) and thus have worth. As if the woman's beauty is something that they owe to men. How often have you heard some variation of, "She's beautiful. She should be flattered by the attention she gets from men." Or "She's beautiful. She should expect that men will be creeps. They can't help it."

If womankind ever sheds its insecurities about looks, the world better watch out.

I am here to challenge all of you, your daughters and nieces, neighborhood women, and future generations of women to take a stand against the exploitation of our hate and shame against our beautiful and natural bodies! Who's with me? For more safe spaces and places to be yourself and come as you are in a self-loving environment, there is a social media platform alternative. Go to kyndr.com and download the app today (See more on this in Chapter K)!

Where do we go from here? Let's say you are reading this and saying it to yourself or your BFF in your book club.

Let me help you with this jumpstart.

First, please stop hating your body. I know there is no magic wand for this, so find one thing to love. Is it your lips or your hips? Is it your eyes or your hair? Perhaps it's your nail beds or skin tone. Find something to love about you, tell a friend, and have her tell you. This is where gay boyfriends are literally the best friends a girl can ever have. These awesome humans will always find things to compliment you on, even on your shittiest hair day. They may also redress you into a color that's way more your season. I'm told that I'm a Winter, whatever that means. All I know is that when they tell me to wear a certain color, fabric, and style, I not only look fab, sisters, I am fab. Bad mood over.

Now, get off toxic social media designed to keep you hooked on the negative crack so that more ad dollars flow to the devil.

Rinse and repeat. Tell three women in your life whom you love, respect, and care about one thing you love and admire about each of their bodies. By starting this positive body image language sequence, you break the cycle of hundreds of years of mistreatment of our image. You must know that saying mean things about our bodies and the bodies of others, affects us all. Even the likes of someone famous and gorgeous and talented and global, like Taylor Swift. Which, are you kidding me? She went from size 00 to size 4 and was criticized at every size. First, she's dying and emaciated, then she's fat. She is neither. She is exactly her beautiful, authentic self. And deserves all the love, support, and gratitude for helping our younger generations to have a positive role model.

Finally, have you ever given thought to the fact that women in many other cultures around the world do not share the ideal of the skinnier, the better? I'm thinking of women struggling to feed their babies in particular. It is a more common issue than we would like to think. Consider them when considering yourself and the self-talk you have with you in the mirror every day. Look at yourself in the mirror and narrow into your beautiful face. Now, look even more closely into your own eyes. I know it feels weird but do it anyway. No one is looking except you. Who do you see? What do you feel? How do you see yourself differently than the usual nitpicking that you do? You feel a little softer, don't you? That's right, be kind to yourself, start here, and say something nice to you. That's how self-love begins and grows from there, and so it goes, and so it goes, and so it goes. Now, you're really onto something beautiful beyond your face and exterior body. You're onto meeting and supporting and loving the real you. Hello you! Where have you been all your life?

The Big So What?

When it comes to loving oneself, no one struggles with this more than women. We women must strive every day to hear kind words about us and say those words to ourselves, even in the quietude of our homes. During COVID, women had it even harder than their male counterparts. Why? The amount of invisible work that loaded onto our already overloaded plates became those platters I've been talking to you about. And, when we are overloaded, there is nothing left to give anyone, let alone ourselves. When we are depleted and out of gas in our tank, we go to the well and come up with fumes. Those fumes are what go to others, not ourselves. We crawl into bed and binge-watch ANYTHING that takes us away from our never-ending reality of heavy lifting. With the breadcrumb left of energy, the only self-love deployed is brushing our teeth. Okay, let's work with that. While brushing your teeth, ideally twice daily, morning and night, I'm a dentist's daughter. I miss my dad, whose dental hygiene habits are instilled in me forever. Thanks, Dr. Bob! I love my pearly whites and my gums that no longer bleed cause I'm actually flossing. Look, Dad, I'm doing it! If that's a self-loving bridge too far, then go ahead and love your smile, your lips, or f-it, go back to your hips and love those too.

T

is for Trust – But Verify

"Being able to put your blinders on, ignore negative opinions, and follow your strong intuition is what's validating to me. It's a great feeling to know you can trust your gut."
—Whitney Wolfe Herd

So, let's get into it as to what's so tricky about trust. Do you trust anyone these days? Even yourself? If not, read on, warrior princesses, read on. Trust is something that is earned, not given. You know it, I know it, we all know it. Yet, we all want it now, right NOW, like immediately. Why? Why can't we cool it a little and let it grow? I'll tell you why. We live in a world of instant gratification instead of the old days when we took our time getting to know a person's vision and values and what makes them tick. Today, we expect it to happen lickety-split. How does this even work? Let's break down the components of trust in a way that most of you aren't even aware of. I'm not being condescending. I teach this for a living to leaders all over the world, men and women, who do not fully understand trust and what to do to earn it and give it, and these people manage thousands of people collectively, maybe more. We have forgotten how to trust—not why, when, where, or with whom. It's the "how" that has us stumped. Let's break it down into bite-sized pieces so you don't get a belly ache or, worse, an ulcer. That's no joke if you've ever had one, and stress does cause them. PERIOD.

Trust is made up of two equal and critical parts. Part I: Competence and Part II: Character. Now, let's look under the covers at both vital parts.

When we stop separating personal from professional and our work selves from our homebody selves, etc., this lack of compartmentalizing is the beginning of openness to trust. We need both parts at work and home, in all space and time, wherever we go, even on vacation, to fully create trusting relationships. Competence is not just for our working situations. Competence is what we are naturally good at and, when possible, what we learn and grow into. Character is our north star of integrity and value system being shared with others, even with ourselves when no one else is looking, and stated and shown in our intentions. Think of it this way: when you are getting to know a co-worker or someone you're dating who is new to you, don't all of these aspects have to apply mutually for trust to grow? Without trust, there is no love, no healthy long-term relationships, and certainly no productive workplace teams. Trust is the foundation of all that we have. As bad as it feels without it, it feels oh so good with it.

When we do things out of our own integrity or best interests, even if we are doing such things for others, this is not being trustworthy for us! And how can you possibly be in a trusting situation with anyone else if you can't even trust yourself? This chapter has such a doomsday feeling. Gotta deal with it, though, so let's go.

The best ways to form trust, the show of it all, lie within you first. Yes, you got it, *me before we* applies here again. It's becoming one of my greatest hits. Put that with my ashes someday and smoke it. Sorry, that was gross. You get the point. Don't you? Maybe not. Let me back this truck all the way up.

There is someone in my life whom I love and care for and know, really know. She does things outside of her value system all the time. She's not a criminal or involved in anything unethical but always lets herself down. She has fantasies about the kind of work she believes she is "supposed" to do and even the type of work she aspires to do, but it is NOT in her area of expertise, let alone within her grasp. Poor thing, she has spent so much money, time, effort, and worrying just to get into this career field that she believes she HAS to go into. And, what's even worse is that some of the closest people to her in her life are urging her to keep going, Nike-style. Just do it!

Cheerleading someone onto something they aren't good at or truly love for themselves is disingenuous and totally out of the trust circle. Boot them out! But no, she keeps going and going, hitting her head and wasting so much energy. The longer this goes, the less she trusts herself. Now, things are murky. She isn't sure this is what she really wants, let alone needs. But will she disappoint all those that she's supposed to be able to rely on and trust? Maybe, but it's time to let go and make a new path if she cannot complete the cycle of being highly competent and in her best self-characteristics within this chosen vocation. Too bad, so sad for those alleged cheerleaders. They nasty!

Now amplify this forward and imagine that she somehow makes it into this field and is struggling to get to work each day, and when at work, she is letting down her co-workers, the boss is all over her ass, and her family and friends are starting to turn on her. This does not bode well for her trusting herself to find the next gig. And now, those she relies on don't trust her either. And in turn, you guessed it, she no longer trusts them. Trust is broken and must start over and be re-earned. The good news is that it is possible to hit refresh or start fresh. This happens all the time. Did you know that in today's society, people change jobs every 3-

5 years and change careers at least three times in a lifetime? This is a new era of the gig economy and rideshare workforce. We work for ourselves as fierce women more and more than for the overlord men of days past. Thank the goddess, can I get an amen? Put your hands up.

The Big So What?

Trust takes time, and it's worth the wait. Start with yourself, then navigate the path outward to those closest and most important to you. Next, you're ready to build trust on a solid foundation you've built at the office and the wine and art nightclub you go to weekly. You have mastered half the equation by establishing trusting ways that stem from positive intent and true integrity on the character side of the house. When it comes to your natural and learned capabilities and ultimate performance ending in results, you are mastering the competence side of things. Well done, you! As you establish how to build trust with others, keep these components in mind and your hearts while you're at it, and go ahead and include your gut—your intuition—which is clearly the secret weapon that women are born with when we honor it. Try these on like a great new pair of shoes or slippers (*slippahs* for my Hawaiian loved ones). Go on, try it. You'll like it. As you establish all the key components that make up full trusting relationships, you'll notice the duality within you and trust yourself, too! And so will they.

Trust is NOT about likability. Just because you like someone does not automatically qualify them as trustworthy.

U

is for Unity – Seek to Understand Before Being Understood

"Yet, dare we be at ease? We are part of a world whose unity has been almost completely shattered. No one can feel free from danger and destruction until the many torn threads of civilization are bound together again. We cannot feel safer until every nation, regardless of weapons or power, will meet together in good faith, the people worthy of mutual association."

—RBG

While this book is not explicitly religious, it is spiritual. If you are a religious woman reading this, that's great. What I am about to teach is a universal principle. Unity is critical for women. We are either the best for each other or the worst. Let's stop settling for tearing one another down and lift each other up! Let's unify. Unity means mind, soul, and body; it also means trinity, trifecta, and hat trick if you are a hockey fan. The triangle effect of things in life keeps happening, doesn't it? Look at the threes in your life. Come on, ladies, just open up to this possibility. Let's dispel the myth that groups of three women will always be challenging and leave someone out. It's simply not true. Middle child syndrome? I don't buy it. Our perception becomes reality, so turn it around and consider the power of three as unity.

For about 20 years, I led hundreds of trainings with teams. The best ways to teach and learn happen in threes. Check this out. You sit in my classroom to learn more effective communication approaches to level up your job. I have you grouped with two other women. One of you works through the communication strategies as the giver, another woman in the group acting as the receiver, and the third lady acting as the observer. Then, over the time we are together, you rotate through all positions until the lesson is complete. Why is this so important? Because we must experience the triangulation of things in order to fully complete the cycle and gain the learning and understanding that results in wisdom. So, in the first round, you practice language that sounds pithy, powerful, and precise. You speak clearly and coherently with enough energy and enthusiasm to keep your receiving party engaged. Their role is to listen actively and openly, listening to connect with you, not control you or step in too early or over you. No interruptions, please; that's the opposite of unification. The observer has a rating card in front of them and is rating each of your respective roles on a 10-point scale. How well did you communicate? How well did she listen? As you go through the three rounds so that each participant experiences the perspective and growing knowledge from the others, the strength of your communication skills amplifies and improves rapidly. To honor unity, you choose real-world scenarios that embrace what you're dealing with at work right now, in particular, challenging situations and people. Before you know it, you feel seen, heard, and understood. Good job!!! This is the power of unity, triangle style. What did The Beatles sing? Oh, I know, "Come together, right now!"

Now, let's focus on one of the greatest support and uplifting systems in the world—women who work with, support, and raise up other women.

Unfortunately, there is the opposite, too—women tearing down other women. To me, there is nothing worse. It's painful to witness, let alone be a part of. Has this happened to you? I hear about it and observe it in my coaching practice, and it's heartbreaking. (For more, check out what I've written about Women vs. Women on my website.)

When Michelle Obama said, "When they go low, we go high," I'm not sure if she meant this for gender specifics since she was referring to bullying. But she's so right. When bullies go low, gender regardless, we must go high. However, this applies to women vs. women too. Taking the high road may not be the path of least resistance or even a natural option in the heat of the battle. Yet, I urge you, I implore you, to take a breath, take a step back over or travel above it all in your imagination, and find another way to choose the light. The light, like the truth, will set you free. By taking the high road, you elevate your position, self-worth, and leadership skills. You lead by example, and others, not only women, will follow what you do, not what you say. That's how great leadership works. Women have it in them to take the high road; we really do. We are so well equipped; we have babies, for goodness sake. We are remarkable beings, with gobs of love to give and emotional intelligence to couple with our Spidey sense. Now, that's a triple threat toward unity.

The Big So What?

Unity is, in its truest sense of the word, a verb. It's an action we take after a decision we make. This is not the time to over think and underplay, let alone play small. We must think big and act bigger if we stand a chance at creating unifying forces for ourselves, our families, and other women. The communal effect of unity on society will stem from women. We will fiercely nurture through where no men have gone before. They ain't birthing no babies, Miss Scarlet.

V

is for Value

"A woman who cannot honor her own feelings will not find them honored by anyone else."
—Marianne Williamson

Value is a two-way street to overly giving hell. Feel me? We women will give and give and give and then give some more until we are totally and completely drained. In this state of depletion, we make poor and uninformed decisions about what to do next. We are coming at life from a place of total disadvantage when this occurs, and much of it we do to ourselves. NOTE: I did not say, and please don't mishear me, that women are totally in charge of this. Societally, the pressure on women is massive. MASSIVE. We are expected to take on all the invisible work in the home, our jobs, kids, the neighbor's kids who need a place to crash after school while we work from home and manage it all, and grocery shop, cook, do laundry and make the entire family's dental appointments. The list of "things" we do may very well fill this entire book, but that would be a horrible read, like a living nightmare. Wait, that's the problem; we are living in society's invented documentary on the real life of overworked women, starring all women, for the most part. Rant over.

So, there is only one way, actually that's fiction, there are only two ways to deal with the value equation for women. First, let's redefine what it means to give value and then redefine what it means to receive value. Then, finally, ensure the equation is harmonious for me, myself, and I.

For example, the value we give at work includes our Effort, Energy and Expertise. These are the three Es! Write these down and really consider the total value you bring to work when you bring it each day.

The value we receive from work, for example, includes Compensation, Confidence-building, and Creativity. These are the three Cs!

Of course, we offer many other attributes in the value equation each day in our jobs, as well as ways to receive thanks, praise, and recognition beyond compensation from that work. This is the value equation. And, once you fully understand it, it's so important that you assess the value you bring and truly understand and measure the value you are receiving. No, I am not talking about nickel and diming or phoning it in and being passive-aggressive. I'm talking about equality! Imagine a world where women are given equal pay for equal work. Now, in the same future state, picture doing work you love and being loved for it beyond your pocketbook. In this type of exchange, you work hard, always have and always will, AND you work SMART. And finally, you are given great pay, benefits, flexibility, and praise for your work. In fact, the value exchange is so clearly equitable that you feel joyful and productive each and every day. In this world, you wake up excited to go to work and finish the day knowing you are valued for all the value you give. Full stop. Work is done (within reason, albeit you have a few emails to check or maybe a social post to launch before bed). Your time off is valued, too, and this is now an everyday occurrence, not just on weekends and vacations. I mean, PTO is personal time off, which is a daily occurrence in this woman's world. Why can't it be true for you!?

The Big So What?

Why is the inequality plaguing most of us today such an issue? Let's say you're highly compensated. Let's also say you give 120% at work and put in ridonculous hours just to stay afloat and ahead of the competition. Aren't you in an upside-down equation that's a never-ending story? They pay you a lot, so you gotta give them all of you so as not to be considered less than, or worse, taken out at the knees by the next willing participant to take your lucrative gig. See, when we are a slave to the almighty dollar, our clarity gets confused. We stare into the funhouse mirror and see how much we "owe" them and must always remain on high octane. When actually, we need to get a grip. There is an exchange that more and more women and even companies today are starting to adopt. It's called pay for performance. Pay is not just money. It's all the good stuff that comes along with the value you're given for your work, such as flex time, a gym membership, extra days off, etc. If you are in an unequal situation, try to right your own ship where you are. Otherwise, you'll want to sail off into the distance to a safer harbor. Ahoy!

W

is for Wait for It – Power of Pause

"Pause-itivity: The power of the pause."
—Eleanor Brownn

W is for wait. Wait for it… W may be my favorite letter in this book. Why? I love the question why! Actually, it's not even a W, it's a P! Confused yet?

Let's take a breath.

Too bad we can't hold our breath for 30 seconds too easily. If you can, that's awesome. Just don't pass out. This chapter is all about the power of pause. It's about waiting! Wait before you leap into saying yes when you really mean no. Wait before you react, or in my case, overreact to something. Wait before you start solving your best friend's life drama. WAIT. It's like "stop in the name of love" because it's super loving to yourself and others when you wait before launching in. We are terrible at this. Why? We can't help ourselves, that's why.

When was the last time you made an amazing decision? Did you wait before you leaped? I bet you did. That's what wise women do. Let's wise up and use this tool that I invented. It's officially called "The Power of Pause."

My best clients are incredible at this. They have repeatedly practiced with me, along with my phone's stopwatch, to pause for 30 seconds before answering questions or solving problems. Try it tonight with someone in your home or over the phone. Pick a topic that is not super critical, like "What will I eat for dinner?"

Picture this: it's 3 p.m., and your workday wraps up around 5 p.m., give or take an hour. It's that time of day when you are getting hungry, yet you don't know what you want. I mean, who has time to even think about that? Hello, fast food! But, no ma'am, not today, you are going to WAIT. Have someone available to time you if something does come to mind. Let's say it's the old standby of grab-and-go fast food that comes up first, immediately. Now, have that full 30 seconds to allow yourself the grace and space to think, feel, smell, and imaginarily taste what it is that you really want. Scan your body and the options. CLICK. The timer goes off, and your best gal says to you, "Okay, time. What do you really crave?" And, you say something to the effect of Whole Foods or the most local and healthy place that has some home cooked-type yummy and healthy and not crazily priced options. YES, that's what you really wanted all along. You had to wait for it to sink in and be fully appreciated, and it only took 30 seconds. Damn, you're good. Now amplify this out into other situations.

This is a great tool to use for really strategic problems that need to be addressed. Let's say out of nowhere, someone is leaving a vacant position at work and your boss asks you to apply for it. Knee-jerk with no waiting, you jump on that. Hell yes, why not? Must be your lucky day! Or is it? Now, take 30 seconds to ponder and really consider the options and if you really want it, and if you don't, what to do about it and how.

For the men in your lives that you love and that love you (brothers, husbands, co-workers, etc.), please encourage us ladies to take that 30 seconds when you ask us to do something or help you. And for the love of mercy, let us do the same with you. Before you launch into not hearing us fully, cause you're listening without hearing, and fix our problems, WAIT! If we really need your help, we'll let you know. Otherwise, we may simply need a resounding "It's going to be ok," …and if you use the power to pause, saying that and meaning it will most likely be enough.

The Big So What?

Over time, with practice, you won't need 30 seconds. You may only need 10. Why do we hate dead space so badly that we talk over it incessantly to avoid any quiet? If you time yourself, you'll realize that 10 seconds is quite long. Take your time, take the time, and make the time, too. Time is precious; it's meant to be savored and cherished. I cherish each of you for trying the power of pause and embracing your WAIT.

X
is for X-factor

"Self-confidence is a superpower that can help determine our success. It is a force that gives us the courage and strength to take any risk, despite knowing our weaknesses. Our leaders play a great role in empowering us, supporting us in rebuilding ourselves and reinventing our self-expression."

—Cardi B

This chapter is a trap, RUN! But keep reading; there is a punchline, and the joke is on us, unfortunately.

I cannot tell you how many times people have told me that I have the X-factor, the "it factor," or all that horseshit. I don't, and none of us do; that's just more pressure to outperform the rest at the cost of ourselves. Right!? I'm so tired of having to live up to other people's standards. As if great isn't good enough, I gotta be Xponential. This is where that survivor stuff comes right back in to haunt us. We are not living our lives in an episode of "Survivor," but it sure seems that way, doesn't it? More illusions. Let's blow those up too. Let's play myth-busters, shall we?

Myth: You gotta be exponentially better than all other women to get ahead.

Myth: You gotta be a triple threat to win.

Myth: You gotta be the best at EVERYTHING you do, or try to do, no matter what, ALWAYS.

You get the point.

My daughters and I love the song *You Gotta Be* by Des'ere (1999 Mix). Yessah! The chorus says,

"You gotta be bad
You gotta be bold
You gotta be wiser
You gotta be hard
You gotta be tough
You gotta be stronger
You gotta be cool
You gotta be calm
You gotta stay together
All I know, all I know
Love will save the day"

So, what's love got to do with it? Well, everything! And as we learned together in Chapter S, self-love is what counts the most. When we love ourselves and reach for our own stars, there is no X-factor. There is a Y-factor. Y stands for YOU! (That's right, Chapter Y is up next, and it's all about YOU.)

There are simply too many "you gottas" in our way. We aspire to the X-factor because we've learned that will get us ahead and keep us there. What is the cost of all that? Is it worth it? Most likely not when you weigh the consequences of going for X. Won't you join me in starting a Y-factor culture for women?

Yes, it's counter to today's high-powered, X-potential culture that drives us all. Isn't it time to try it a different way? Let's turn things on their head and soften them. Soft does not equal weak. Soft equals loving, cushioned, and lovely. It's the thing that becomes the superpower of truly successful women who are living the lives they've always dreamed of and never dared to try until now. If you are contemplating giving up the X and trading in that eXhausted way of living, you are not alone. Today, millions of women are working differently and better by putting their own needs first and suffering no fools telling them that they're wrong or scaring them that this approach will hurt them and the ones they love most.

Fear has no business making decisions. Fear will lie to you. Why? Because of that whole thing about its acronym. It's true! FEAR is False Evidence Appearing Real. Living as an X-factor female is driven partly by the villain in this story, FEAR. What's that you say? The opposite of FEAR is Courage! Damn straight it is.

There is no courage without vulnerability. Brené Brown has done a BRILLIANT job proving this with her PhD-level research. And where there is vulnerability, there is fear; it's natural. And no amount of X in your factors will eradicate it. A little fear is healthy, but panic kills. Any surfer in the world will tell you that. So, what are you left to do? Embrace the fear, look at it straight in its face, and ask what it is trying to tell you. And answering firmly yet calmly, "No, thank you, fear." I'll take it a little slower today to honor my why.

The Big So What?

If you are currently working at a fever pace and "known" for being the woman who has it all, you most likely are suffering from X-factor syndrome. Man, it's exhausting. Did men invent this crap? Let's burn it with our 1960s feminine fatales like heels and bras. They did not invent Rosie the Riveter to create the X-factor for all of us to live up to and then, while we're at it, lap her like a racecar and set new world records that take X to X to X. And, for the nerds in all of us, yours truly included, the real issue is what we women have done to create an unsustainable pace like a speeding train. It looks like this: $factor^x$. Get it? Our skills, abilities and expertise put up to the factor of exponential is a way to keep us running hard and fast inside that same old hamster wheel. Yup, you heard me. You're now back to sprinting inside of marathons while balancing on teeter totters for months, maybe years on end. Oh, and they "love" us for it, right? All the theys. While we hate ourselves. Talk about opposites that don't attract or stay together. It's time to shed the X. Focus on your Y (and your why). Purpose is so primal to existence. What is your ultimate purpose? Why are you here? That's where you want to spend the most time, effort, and energy, isn't it? I'll be your fairy godmother from now on. POOF. You have permission.

Y
is for YOU!

"Examine what you tolerate.
What you put up with, you end up with.
What you allow continues.
Reevaluate the costs and your worth."
—Karen Salmansohn

This is such a wonderful time to be YOU. There is only one you, and you are your biggest fan and your own best friend when you allow yourself the freedom to focus on yourself. It is NOT selfish; it is selfless to act this way. You already know that this is the only way to be truly joyful, a contributing member of society, and there for your kids, friends, and loved ones. There is and forever and always will only be one you, just like your fingerprints—they are yours and yours alone.

Look at it this way: if you see life as a gem, maybe a diamond in the rough, you will cherish yourself. All around you are opportunities and choices as to how you spend your days and years. You must choose to spend life's poker chips by making bets that will pay off. Sometimes this is short-term and other times long-term. Look around these beautiful facets: your career, family, friends, community, and wellbeing. Blend them up cocktail style or ala carte. Some days, 10 hours will go to sleep. Delicious! Rare, yet so good. Other days, work is at a 12 and sleep a six, mixing in three hours for self-care and three for the dogs. That's a cool day, too. Mixing and matching how we spend time in honor of our best selves is how to honor the best of you. YOU COUNT. You were born for a reason. Together, we will continue to explore what you're here for and how to get in alignment with what it is that you really want.

When is the last time you recall hearing another woman talk about what she wants? What she really, really wants. Remember? No? Okay, try now. Ask your bestie what she wants. Have her really allow herself to go there and answer this question from deep inside her soul. Then have her ask you. Go for it; really dive in. What did you come up with?

The greatest women of history, in the modern day and whomever she is in the future, will have had to ask themselves this question and answer it. This is multiple choice, you know. Our calling is our mission, and our missions may change with the times and circumstances we find ourselves in.

Whether we consider Madame Curie and her invention of the polio vaccine or Maya Angelou and her gift of prose that enlightens and empowers us while teaching us what it is like to be a woman of color on this planet, we are thankful, grateful, and so much more ourselves as women because they honored their own true selves.

The Big So What?

You will never know if you don't try. That's a fact. Whether you wanted to be an astronaut (I coach several rocket scientists who are remarkable women), or a culinary artist iron chef style, a stay-at-home mom, or a poet, you must consider what's best for you. And only you. THEN and only then is it time to consider the impact on and to others. Remember to start with your inner most circle, your ride-or-die people. Not just immediately family, the closest circle of friends and allies. Does your moonshot help or hurt them? It helps, right? There you go, so keep going with it; now that's the way. By exploring what makes you great and makes you filled with glee, there is no doubt you will succeed and help others, too. You will lead the way, light the path, and shine as bright as a diamond. We are all like carbon, turning into the diamonds of our dreams.

Z
is for the Zone

"Remember, you have been criticizing yourself for years and it hasn't worked. Try approving of yourself and see what happens."
—Louise L. Hay

I have been teaching, or attempting to teach, this for over 30 years! OUCH—that makes me realize my age, not in a bad way either, but in a way that's revealing. Being in the zone is all about playing complex chess on the board of life. I learned this concept so long ago I may botch the original. No Botox required. I don't want a permanent look of surprise. Just give me some grace and work with me. The old-school version of the zone was known as the "lens of understanding." It was actually pretty cool for a first-time people manager in my very early 20s. It taught me that you have to get along with people. And seek to also get appreciated by people. And, of course, you must also get things done, lots of lots of things. Oh, and don't forget! To be truly masterful, you must also get things right. Easy-peasy right? SO wrong. So very, very wrong. Back then, I died trying. No one ever explained it to me the way I will explain it to you now.

Today, we need to master multidimensional chess at work. That's for certain. It is a time of extreme complexity, hyper-competition, and globalization. That does not mean "outworking" everyone else. It's a surefire way to exhaustion, sickness, and a mental breakdown. Been there and done ALL of that. It means mastering the board. Life is a game, after all. Do you want to be a pawn?

So, what the hell do you do with all of this? It sounds near impossible, doesn't it? Kind of. It's tough. This zone will require you to abandon old thoughts and beliefs around what it takes to be masterful.

It will also require that you open yourself up to new interpretations of working and being and playing and relaxing. Paradigm shift. Hell yeah.

The zone is being in all four quadrants at one time. In the zone at home with the fam, you are on the same wavelength with everyone while being appreciated by them and getting a bunch of stuff done strategically and effectively. What a friggin' rock star you are. And remember, rock stars like Stevie Nicks live forever and perform for a lifetime. Superstars burn out. What happened to Lipps Inc. who had the one-hit wonder "Funkytown"? Burnout most likely. They fell out of the zone.

Now, it is true that many of us wonderful women are great at occupying two of these four critical life areas at one time without really trying. How many of you reading this can get to three? It takes time, effort, energy, trade-offs, and knowledge of where you are, where you have been, and where you are headed, along with what lies ahead. It's hard! It is something that you can learn. I teach it to powerful women every day.

Once you master three of the four areas of the zone, then you may join the place few of us occupy, by living and spending time, effort and energy within all four areas. This is where the best, most juicy, and awe-inspiring days exist. We up level to all four. Here is a beautiful day where you feel great in your relationships, you are getting things done that take the least amount of effort and product the biggest bang for your buck. Here you are also appreciated by others who see and experience the real you and finally, you are on top of your day, checking off open items one after the other; energized by the entire sequence instead of the usual depletion and binge-watching that occurs.

Now, which area, whether you're reading this chapter first or you've read all the other chapters and are at the end of this book, do you believe is the hardest for women to practice, establish and conquer? Which area do you avoid? Which area feels really hard for you? Since we are women, the answer most likely is:

Get appreciated. Who has time? Make the time ladies, because if you don't, others won't. And that's the bottom line.

The Big So What?

How do you practice getting appreciated without making yourself nauseous? You pay it forward. Don't you appreciate other women all the time? You say it out loud, don't you; it's called a thank you! Thank you, Betty, for covering my shift while I was home with a sick kid. Thank you, Kanesha, for reaching out to me after I cried in the bathroom at work today. Thank you, Cherie, for asking about my ill father-in-law. The thank yous that you bestow upon other women are not only good graces or etiquette. Screw that. You are truly grateful from the bottom of your heart, aren't you? So, why not feel that gratitude yourself? Ladies, you take the gift away when someone praises you in honest gratitude. Accept it. Allow its goodness to pierce the armor that guards your heart. By paying it backward and forward, you will stop keeping score and start feeling better, more loved, maybe even cherished. This feeling of being appreciated will seep into all you do and, most importantly, into all you are.

Thank you from the bottom of my heart for reading this book, trying these new concepts, and challenging yourselves to grow. My favorite quote since I was a little girl with a blind sister says,

---

"Alone we can do so little; together so much."

—Helen Keller

Acknowledgments

How do I thank many people, especially women, who have supported me in this endeavor to launch this book as a mission? THANK YOU! With my deepest gratitude, you fill my cup and provide me with joy and insights each and every day. To the women in my coaching practice, both one-on-one and group, who were brave enough and on mission to the degree that they felt compelled to share their stories, battles, and breakthroughs, you are why I do what I do. This includes, but in no way is limited to Betsy Kamalei, Kainoa, Nina, Sara, Jasmeet, Anita, and so many others who wished to remain anonymous. I respect and thank each and every one of you.

For my dearest Sonia Naneaonalani, you are the world's greatest gift of a human to me in all the crazy endeavors we have chosen to launch into with work and way beyond, sometimes ass first 😊 over the past eight years. You are truly the wind beneath my wings and the period to my ever-lasting run-on sentences. Your talents are numerous and sometimes misunderstood, even by yourself, so please continue to reach for your own stars while co-creating magic for authentic humans with me. You are officially hānai to me (more or less informally adopted, the Hawaiian way).

Shoutout must go to my augmented team of additional supportive and brilliant creatives, Bea, Shaina, Ella, and Jupiter; I have endless gratitude.

To all the incredible women who have gone before me to establish their places in herstory as leaders, muses, and crusaders, we have done our best throughout the A-Z chapters to highlight your greatness with your quotes. We chose each and every one of these quotes by design. You have, and for some, posthumously, will continue to inspire us into action and clarify our why into purpose. My heart is full of the light you shine.

And a major shout out to the endorsing blurbists. Can you believe that this is what these meaningful quotes inside of book covers (and sometimes on the front and outside) are called? Blurbs. From the bottom of my heart, I know how busy you are, and you took the time to digest my manuscript when I needed the fuel injection of your genius most. Laura Vanderkam, Erin Gallagher, Marsha Williams, Daisy Auger-Dominguez, Jupiter Stone, and Karen Salmansohn. You simply ROCK!!!

And now to Michelle Kulp. What would I do without you? Your publishing prowess, guidance, design team (shoutout Zeljka for the incredible cover), and editorial staff have made this book what it was born to be. Mahalo Nui Loa Heather! Without your method, experience, and confidence-instilling support, I'm not sure that I would have went for it, exposing myself fully and openly to the world of women as the face of the anti-burnout movement.

Finally, to my forever and ongoing staff of fur babies, you are the best co-workers ever, despite the ongoing need for treats and potty breaks, you remind me to give myself a break too. The meditative state of petting you makes me more joyful before I start my day, so let's keep that morning ritual going, no matter what. Love you Lily Rose, Leilani, Leo, Mochi and Jojo. Also known as the mutley crew.

And to my human family. Darren La'akea, you continue to support me, hold space for me, and allow me to be my best and highest self. Your ability to expand yourself as my husband, soul-father to our daughters, and now a leader at your work is truly wonderful to witness and be a part of. I need that free space on my life's bingo card to do what I do and how I do it, which is challenging, and you wanted that! :) Love you with my highest self, truly and deeply. Keep reminding me "that it will be ok" and so it is! Men can really learn from you how to partner, father, and friend...

Ava Jodi, you are always ready, as my eldest, to dive in head first into whatever topic I want to explore, and then, you add to it with an empathic heart, whether on the phone or coming onto my podcast, you're always ready to jump in to honor others with your own lessons! Keep crusading for those less fortunate and continue to accomplish your own ways of keeping burnout at bay. Jiu-jitsu is your art and your science. I'm so proud of you for all that you've accomplished and will continue to pursue. In your quest for love and partnership, you're on track, your own magnificent track, so stay on it, true to yourself. Finally, in your career endeavors, you have chosen a bumpy road, however, just know this, you are not settling, nor are you giving up, and for that, you are building life's muscle towards a vocation that's sure to be filled with joy, productivity, and value. These are the interrelated vitals that I teach in this book and that you're starting to take hold of in flight. Keep soaring! Love your light and your gifts, keep unwrapping them. I adore you.

Annika Kahea Raye, you are no doubt my mini-me in the best of ways and yet, the toughest ones also. Duality prevails. If I knew at your young womanhood age what you are exploring and mastering now, I would have written this book decades ago. You, my dearest, are on a vision quest that represents what I wish for in all women and marginalized people throughout the world. You are the purest definition of mind, soul, body, spirit, and emotional intelligence, working together for the greater good of yourself first and then and, therefore, others. May I continue to be a support system for you as a woman who has made many mistakes and learned from them to become a mirror for you as a reflection of what's to come, which is your very best and highest self, emerging, growing, transforming, and ascending! Your star shines bright with your gifts of singing, cooking, and exploring the world. Can't wait to be a witness to what you co-create next, you are a magic and major manifester. I adore you.

My hanai mama, Susie Leimakamei, you are remarkable, let's just say over the age of 80, you know who you are and act so selflessly when others are in need of your cooking, paintings, ear or shoulder, and so much more, you are the epitome of what you told me because you show me and other women around the world, how to be your own best friend. I'm forever grateful that you came into our lives and that our journey has led us to the most magical of places as we continue to live Ohana style. I love your heart and how you show up with so much gusto!!!

And to my mainland sisterhood, you've been both an ongoing well of inspiration and a source of belief in me that is humbling and empowering at the same time. Tam Moana, Jill, Barbara, Meta, Em, Amira and Ginny, how do I love thee, let me count the ways… gotta keep this book under 200 pages, so I'm stopping here.

Finally, to the women (and men) of the island of Kauai who have accepted me. My Hawaiian heart continues to learn, grow, and become more unified with a simpler and more sustainable time. As indigenous people everywhere can attest, from the struggle of stolen language, land, and culture, the best way to perpetuate comes from a collaborative community and paying tribute and honor to the lineage, protocols, and ecosystems of the past where things were truly in alignment with nature, spirit, and deep and historical family values. I now feel seen, heard, and understood. This list is not inclusive yet, I must mention Sandi, Ruby, Genn, Kainani, Kresta, Kelly, Mi*key, Courtney & Kumu Troy. With the final mahalo going to my sister from another mister, the incomparable J. Kauilani MitaAra Kahelekai. (Kaui) Whether co-leading retreats, honoring those who have passed, blessing hales (Hawaiin word for home) and the future with our shared ike (Hawaiin word for knowledge) and wisdom, you are simply the gift that keeps on giving. I learn from you each day and am a better and more in tune, Wahine (Hawaiin word for woman), because of how we navigate these deep waters together. Somehow, you've unlocked something inside of me that allows me to see clearly, feel deeply, and experience the true meaning of a life lived in rich purpose for myself and our tribe and now, many, many others and more to come as we take the spirit of aloha and its rooted teachings into the rest of the world for women who are burned out, everywhere. I love you.

(Jodi Nan Look, you taught me how to put oneself first. I wish you were still on this earth with me to celebrate my official growing up as the woman I am today, which you set into motion when I was born as your only sister/sibling. When you passed at the mere age of 25, I was 20, and I knew so little of how to treat myself. I thank you for your boldness and your vehement independence as a fighter and totally blind person navigating in the world of obstacles and beauty. You "saw" something within me that took decades to bloom. Now, I am blossoming, and this book will help thousands of burned-out women around the world to do the same)

Made in the USA
Middletown, DE
15 October 2024